POWER
THROUGH
TRUTH

Practical Applications for Your Life

LOUIE VAN GRENINGER

Louie Von Greninger 11-3-19

ISBN 978-1-0980-0183-4 (paperback)
ISBN 978-1-0980-0184-1 (digital)

Christian Faith Publishing, Inc.
832 Park Avenue
Meadville, PA 16335
www.christianfaithpublishing.com

Printed in the United States of America

Author's Notes

The information in this book represents thirty-seven years of study and research into the following: the spiritual and mental world we all live in, the *King James Version* and *Revised Standard Version Bibles,* and metaphysics. Working as a hairstylist, I have spent fifty-five years with the general public. My clients have ranged from the ultrarich to the basic blue-collar worker. Also I have practiced my trade in a retirement community, as well as working in salons in Oklahoma, Ohio, Arizona, Florida, and California. The insight I have gained by working with people all of these years has been invaluable in writing this book. It is my hope that the information contained within will take the reader from the material world and place him or her into the spiritual and mental world, the real realm in which we all should live.

Acknowledgments

It is with sincere gratitude that I acknowledge Linda Neal Reising for her contribution to this project, transforming it into book form, as well as editing. I also give sincere thanks to my late wife, Virginia, for her support. I dedicate this book to everyone who is interested in improving his or her life by applying the truth.

Louie V. Greninger

Contents

The Universe We Live In

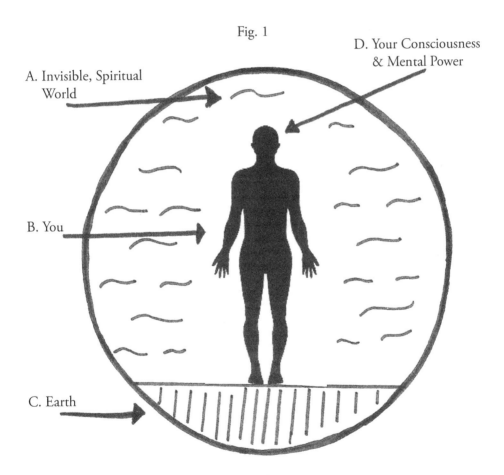

Fig. 1

A. Invisible, Spiritual World

B. You

C. Earth

D. Your Consciousness & Mental Power

Millions of people go through life suffering from illness, depression, and poverty. They lack the knowledge and understanding of the world they live in—the real world—which is invisible, spiritual, and mental. Few people truly understand this. Jesus Christ walked on this earth over 2,000 years ago, trying to show people that the real world is spiritual from beginning to end. Also, people need to realize that the words we speak help create our own reality.

A.

The real universe is invisible—spiritual and mental. You have a physical body (flesh) and a spiritual body (soul). The spirit flows in you and around you.

B. and C.

You are in between the spirit world and the earth, as well as the material world which you can see, smell, and touch.

D.

You are connected to both the spiritual and the material world through your mental consciousness and the other mental powers within you.

Over the years, the interpretation of Scripture has become somewhat confusing. Many years ago, I took a Dale Carnegie course, along with thirty-nine other participants. In one class, the instructor gave a card to a student in the first row. That student was told to silently read the story printed on the card then whisper what it said to the person sitting next to him. The second student was supposed to whisper the story to the person next to him and so on until all forty of us had participated. At the end, the instructor asked the last student to stand and tell the story out loud. Finally, the instructor read aloud what was printed on the card. The story had changed so much, none of us could recognize the original. The Dale Carnegie experiment used only forty people. Just imagine thousands of people over many centuries telling the same story about the world in which we live. You can see how confusing the information might become.

To remove some of the confusion, we need to go back to the beginning of the Bible to help you build a foundation and to provide some understanding of the world in which you live. Just imagine that you and I are in space. It is pitch black as in Fig. A.

Fig. A   Fig. B

Then, as in Fig. B, we hear the voice of God say, "Let there be light and there was light, and God said that the light was good, and God separated the light from the darkness." God created the universe and everything in it by speaking only positive words.

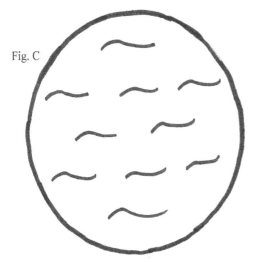

Fig. C

The universe is spiritual and controlled by Divine Intelligence. Scientists say that everything is in vibration and is made up of electrons and protons (energy). The universe, then, has both a positive and a negative side to it. This is very important to you because it has a direct effect on your life as you go on your journey

The universe is spiritual, and God spoke His word into an invisible substance that makes things out of itself. According to Hebrews 11:3, "By faith we understand that the world was created by the Word of God, so that what is seen was made out of things which do not appear." Then God said, "Let us make man in our image after our likeness."

Let's examine that last statement and see how it applies to you.

1. God is spirit—you are spiritual.
2. God is eternal—the real you is eternal.
3. God's spoken word is creative—your spoken word is creative.

Laws and Principles

The real world is invisible and governed by laws and principles. I grew up on a farm near Afton, Oklahoma. It is a perfect place to demonstrate how the laws and principles of life work. For example, if you plant a seed of corn in the soil, by law, it will grow. And by principle, it will reproduce corn after its kind.

This is true with regard to every kind of seed, tree, animal, bird, and person, every living thing. They all reproduce after their kind; that is the law and principle of life. This is where you fit into the creation. By law and principle, the words you speak, be they positive or negative, will reproduce after their kind in due time.

Example A:

Love (Positive)	If you think love, you get love.
Hate (Negative)	If you think hateful thoughts, you get hate.

Example B:

Positive	I am full of joy.
Negative	I am depressed and unhappy.

Ignorance of the laws and principles of life does not excuse you from its consequences. Cause and effect will be discussed in more detail throughout this book.

The Principle of Life

The principle of life that sustains all living things is the eternal here and now.

Example C:

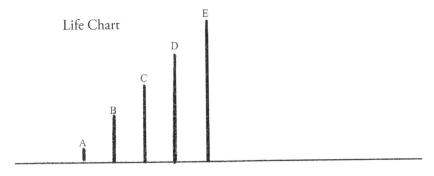

Life Chart

A. The average lifespan of a human (men, 78 years; women, 81 years)
B. The oak tree at Oak Alley (over 350 years)
C. Redwood trees in California (over 2,000 years)
D. A cypress tree in Florida (over 3,000 years)
E. The spruce in the Sierra in California (over 4,000 years)

Now I have a question for you. When was there ever a lack of life? Never.

The Universe

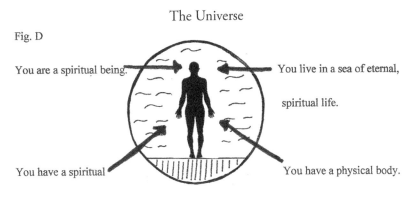

Fig. D

You are a spiritual being.

You live in a sea of eternal, spiritual life.

You have a spiritual body and soul.

You have a physical body.

The Law and Principle of Life flows through you. You are a spirit with a spiritual and a physical body. According to Corinthians: 15-44, if there is a physical body, there is also a spiritual body.

You Are Born of God

You are born of God. You come from the invisible (spiritual) world on one side into a material world on the other side (earth).
Example:

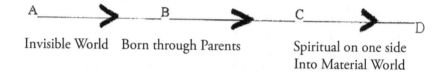

Invisible World   Born through Parents   Spiritual on one side
                                           Into Material World

A. You are born of God. You come from the invisible spiritual world.
B. You are born through your parents, your guardians here on earth.
C. You enter with the spiritual world on one side of you.
D. You come into a material world on earth.

You live and move in a sea of eternal spirit that is in you, through you, and around you.

Universal Polarity

There is a cosmic law of polarity. You see this in the battery you use in your car, inside the cell phone you carry with you, and within the fire alarms you install in your home. The battery has both positive and negative poles. The spirit that flows through your body has both a negative and a positive side to it too. If you want to see how the spirit flows through your body, read any book on acupuncture which uses spirit energy. The truth is the word you speak, and this spirit can have both a positive and negative effect on your life.

Example:

Your	Positive	Love	Strong	I am youthful, etc.
Word	Negative	Hate	Weak	I am getting older, etc.

Your word will reproduce after its kind in due time. That is the law and principle of life.

Terminology

To help to remove any confusion about terminology you may come across, let's go back to the beginning, and you will see that there was nothing until God spoke everything into existence. All things came from the invisible into the visible; therefore, the universe is spiritual, controlled by an infinite intelligence.

"So out of the ground the Lord God formed everything, beast of the field and every bird of the air and brought them to the man to see what he would call every living creature, and that was its name" (Genesis 2:19, King James Version). A scientist in a particular field of work might substitute the word *spirit* with *energy* or *current*. Whatever terminology might be used in various books or papers, just remind yourself that in the Bible, it is called spirit. Throughout this book, you will find different terms used to explain the same thing by using a different name. As long as you realize that you are spiritual and that the universe is spiritual, you will keep yourself on solid ground.

Summary of the World in Which You Live

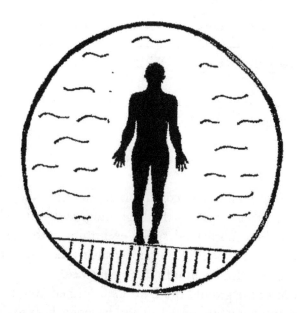

1. The real world is invisible, spiritual, and eternal.
2. You live in a spiritual world on one side of you and the material world on the other.
3. The universe is governed by law and principle.
4. You live in a mental and spiritual world.
5. You are a spiritual being.
6. The world was created by God's spoken word; and you will create your own life and world by your spoken word, whether positive or negative.
7. There is a law of attraction.
8. Every living thing comes from the invisible to the visible, including you.
9. The universe has a polarity, both a negative and positive side to it.
10. There is a principle of life that flows through you and is eternal now.
11. In spirit, there is no time. It only exists in the material side of life.

12. The word of the Lord abides in the world forever.
13. Ignorance of the law and principle of life does not excuse you from the consequences.
14. Everything reproduces after its kind, including the word you speak.
15. "Then Peter opened his mouth and said, 'Of a truth I perceive that God is no respecter of persons'" (Acts 10:34, King James Version). That means that every person alive is controlled by the same law and principle of life.
16. "The fear of the Lord is the beginning of knowledge" (Proverbs 1:7, King James Version). Sometimes the word *lord* is interpreted as *law*.

You Live in a Spiritual, Mental, and Physical Garden

When you read the Scripture, always remind yourself that the information is about you personally, not only think about the information but also apply it now. We are talking about the truth; what was true 5,000 years ago is also true now. And 1,000 years from now, the truth will still be the same.

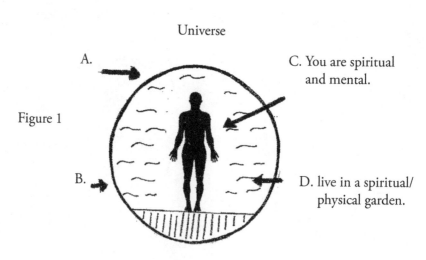

Figure 1

A. The Universe is spiritual, mental, and physical.
B. The Universe is created with both a negative and a positive side.
C. You are spiritual and mental.
D. You live in a spiritual garden now.

The universe has two sides to it, and you are in the middle. You have the indivisible, spiritual, and mental side which is in you, through you, and around you. On the other side, you have your physical body and material world.

(King James Version) Genesis 2:16-17
"And the Lord commanded the man saying, Of every tree of the garden thou mayest freely eat: But of the tree of the knowledge of good and evil thou shalt not eat of it: for in the day that thou eatest thereof thou surely die."

The Tree of Knowledge of Good and Evil

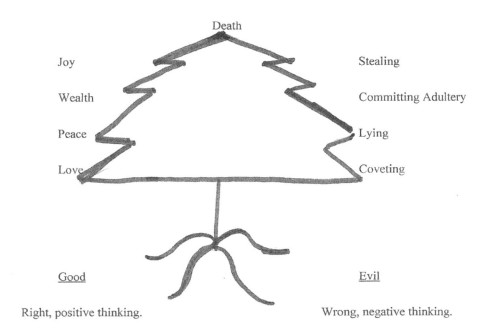

Death

Joy   Stealing

Wealth   Committing Adultery

Peace   Lying

Love   Coveting

Good   Evil

Right, positive thinking.   Wrong, negative thinking.

A Mental Tree of Good and Evil

There was also a Tree of Life in the midst of the Garden.

Spiritual and Mental Tree of Life

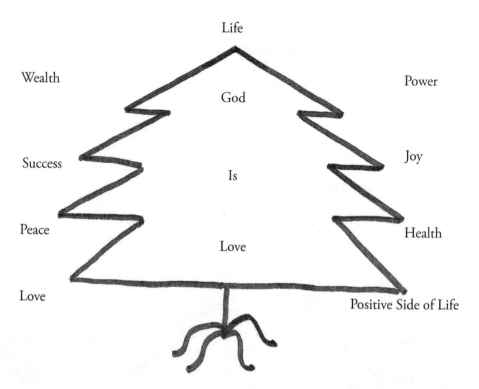

The only way to this tree is through God, by following His word through righteousness, positive thinking, and action. When you eat from this tree of good and evil, you are mixing positive thinking with negative thinking or committing wrong actions.

Example:

Positive	Love	Success	Health
Negative	Hate	Lies	Adultery

When you mix positive with negative thinking over a period of time, you are doing harm to yourself. You are going against the way the universe, and you were created to function.

The Tree of Knowledge of Good and Evil

When Adam and Eve ate the fruit (mental fruit) from the tree of knowledge of good and evil, the Bible does not tell us what type of fruit it was. But Adam introduced sin and evil to people. He also brought into the world negative thinking and talking, as well as wrong actions, which brought death to humans. "So he drove out the man: and he placed at the east of the Garden of Eden cherubim and a flaming sword which turned every way to keep the way of the tree of life" (Genesis 3:24, King James Version).

Scripture: the fruit of the righteousness is a tree of life

A gentle tongue is a tree of life. "Death and Life are in the power of the tongue, and those who love it will eat its fruit" (Proverbs 18:21, King James Version). From the fruit of his mouth, a man is satisfied. The Bible is your spiritual and mental guide. However, it will only benefit you if you read it and apply the information in your daily life. The guidance found there will help lead you back to the tree of life.

Example:

When the road system was created, the builders constructed two sides to the road.

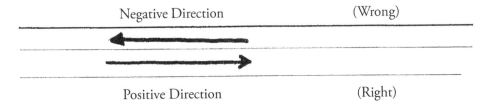

| Negative Direction | (Wrong) |
| Positive Direction | (Right) |

The road was built for you to drive on the right side of the road, at least in the United States. However, you have free will to drive wherever you want. But if you drive on the negative side of the road, you could harm or even kill yourself if you stay there too long. The universe and you were created to function a certain way, just like that road.

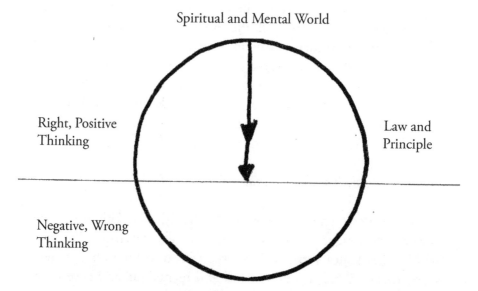

Spiritual and Mental World

Right, Positive Thinking

Law and Principle

Negative, Wrong Thinking

God is good, rightness, power, and positivity. The law and principle of life runs through you, and that is how you are created to function. Think only on the positive side of life. When you think negatively, you are going the wrong way, and you are blocked from God and His power to help you. If you think on the negative side of life, you will create all kinds of problems for yourself because you have separated yourself from God's source of power.

Summary:

1. You live in a mental, spiritual, and physical body, as well as inside the material garden.
2. When you mix negative and positive thinking, you are eating from the mental tree of knowledge of good and evil.
3. Adam introduced sin, evil, and death into the race of man when he ate from the mental tree of good and evil. He did this by negatively thinking, talking, and acting.

4. You were barred from the tree of life by Adam's negative actions.
5. You live in a universe that has both a positive and a negative side to it. Also it contains the law and principle of life, which runs through you. Think, talk, and act on the positive side of life only.
6. The Bible is your spiritual guide here on earth. It would be wise for you to read and study the Bible so you will know what is right and wrong for you.

The Ten Commandments

And God spoke all these words, saying,

I am the Lord thy God, which have brought thee out of the land of Egypt, out of the house of bondage.

Thou shalt have no other gods before me.

Thou shalt not make unto thee any graven images or any likeness of anything that is in heaven above, or that is in the earth beneath, or that is in the water under the earth.

Thou shalt not bow down thyself to them, nor serve them: for I the Lord thy God am a jealous God, visiting iniquity of the fathers upon the children unto the third and fourth generation of them that hate me;

And shewing mercy unto thousands of them that love me, and keep my commandments.

Thou shalt not take the name of the Lord thy God in vain; for the Lord will not hold him guiltless that taketh his name in vain.

Remember the Sabbath day, to keep it holy.

Six days shalt thy labour, and do all thy work:

But the seventh day is the Sabbath of the Lord thy God; in it thou shalt not do any work, thou, nor thy son, nor thy daughter, thy manservant, nor thy maidservant, nor thy cattle, nor thy stranger that is within thy gates:

For in six days the Lord made heaven and earth, the sea, and all that in them is, and rested the seventh day; wherefore the Lord blessed the Sabbath day, and hallowed it.

Honour thy father and thy mother; that thy days may be long upon the land which the Lord thy God giveth thee.

Thou shalt not kill.

Thou shalt not commit adultery.

Thou shalt not steal.

Thou shalt not bear false witness against thy neighbor.

Thou shalt not covet thy neighbor's home, thou shalt not covet thy neighbor's wife, nor his ox, nor his ass, nor anything that is thy neighbor's.

And all the people saw the thunderings, and the lightnings, and the noise of the trumpet, and the mountain smoking: and when the people saw it, they removed, and stood afar off.

And they said unto Moses, Speak thou with us, and we will hear; but let not God speak with us, lest we die.

And Moses said unto the people, Fear not: For God is come to prove you, and that his fear may be before your faces, that you sin not. (Exodus 20:1–20, King James Version)

The Ten Commandments are laws you are not to break. They are put in place for instruction to guide you and to protect you. They also help keep you on the positive side of life and help lead you back to the mental tree of life. God's name is I Am. When you use "I am" in your life, you are using God's name and power in whatever you say.

Example:

I am happy. I am youthful. I am successful. I am full of life.

25

Always use your "I am" in a positive way if you want positive results.

It would be wise to read and study the Bible so you will know what is right and wrong in God's eyes. You are to put nothing before God—not your "I am," not your wife, husband, and children, not drugs and alcohol, not work, not anything that is negative in thought, speech, or action. Because God is good, rightness and positivity are necessary to follow His ways.

God commands that we are not to take His name in vain. Let me remind you that you live in a spiritual and mental world with a positive and a negative side to it. God is saying to you, if you are using his name, I Am, in a negative way, you are using His name in vain. For example, if you say, "I am sick. I am broke. I am getting old. I am unhappy," you are living on the negative side of life. Don't blame God for the results you get. God's power is always on the positive side of life.

You are also to "honor thy father and thy mother: that thy days may be long upon the land which the Lord thy God giveth thee" (Genesis 20:12). You are to honor your earthly parents. They are your guardians on earth. Your real father and mother are encompassed in God, who created the heavens and the earth.

"And God said, Let us make man in our image, after our likeness: and let them have dominion over the fish of the sea and over the fowl of the air and over the cattle and over all the earth and over every creeping thing that creepeth upon the earth" (Genesis 1:26, King James Version). You are made in the image of God. That means:

1. God is spirit; and you, His son or daughter, is also spiritual.
2. God is eternal, and the spiritual you is also eternal.
3. The words God spoke were creative. The words you speak are creative.
4. God spoke the world into existence, and you have the power to speak your world into existence.

It is important that you understand that God is your father and mother. God can help you regenerate your life. This will be discussed more fully in the book as you travel back to the mental tree of life.

"Thou shalt not covet thy neighbour's house, thou shalt not covet they neighbour's wife nor his manservant, nor his maidservant, nor his ox nor his ass, nor anything that your neighbor has" (Exodus 19:17, King James Version). You are to look to God for whatever you need. Also, you are to seek the kingdom of God within yourself.

As you travel down the spiritual road of life, think of each commandment as a mental sign to help you stay on the positive side of life, to instruct you, to guide you, and to protect you in your everyday life. The Ten Commandments are not meant to restrict you but rather to free you and to help you avoid many problems. If you watch the five-o'clock news each day, you will find that most of the people in trouble with the law have broken one or more of the Ten Commandments. If you have children, it would be wise to teach them that they are spiritual and mental. Also they must learn that the commandments will help them avoid serious issues and protect them if they apply the teachings to their daily lives.

A person I will call Jean was being interviewed by a television reporter about the Ten Commandments. Jean stated that the Ten Commandments were outdated for the society of today, and they should be updated to reflect how society currently thinks. Jean most certainly did not understand the world she lived in. Also she did not comprehend her own mental and spiritual powers. The Ten Commandments are eternal. They cannot be changed.

It is the mental belief of society that has drifted away from the truth. You are controlled by laws and principles that flow through you. These cannot be changed. You either work with the laws and principles or against them.

> A man will reap what he sows. (Galatians 6:7, King James Version)
>
> The fear of the Lord [Law] is the beginning of Knowledge. (Proverbs 1:7, King James Version)
>
> The fear of the Lord [Law] leads to life; and he that has it rests satisfied; he will not be visited by harm. (Proverbs 19:23, King James Version)

Because you cannot see the law does not mean that it is not there and that there is no consequence for your actions. You cannot see gravity, but it is there.

Summary:

1. The Ten Commandments are God's laws that cannot be changed.
2. The Ten Commandments are for instruction, guidance, and protection.
3. Any time you use God's name (I Am) in negative thought, speech, or action, you are using God's name in vain.
4. You are not to have any other gods before God. Read the Bible so you will know what is good and evil.
5. The Ten Commandments, if applied, will help to keep you on the positive side of life.
6. God is your real father and mother because you are a spiritual being. Your father and mother on earth are your guardians.
7. You are spiritual, made in the image of God. That means your word is creative. Speak only on the positive side of life.
8. God is eternal; you are eternal.
9. You are not to covet but seek God for what you need.
10. The universe is controlled by law and principle that runs through you. By your spoken word, you either work with the law and principle or against it.

Your Mental Powers

As a man thinketh in his heart, so is he. (Proverbs 23:7, King James Version)

I have worked with the general public for over fifty-five years. My clients have come from different education and income levels, as well as from varied types of communities across the country. Experience has taught me that very few people have any knowledge of their mental powers. In fact, most use their mental powers against themselves. Some simply do not care to explore the mental and spiritual aspects of their own lives.

You are spiritual, made in the image and likeness of God. In fact, the word you speak is creative, governed by law and principle. You are master of your own fate because only you can control your thoughts. It would be wise to learn as much as you can about your mental powers since they are working 24/7 for you or against you.

Your Mental Faculty and Accessory

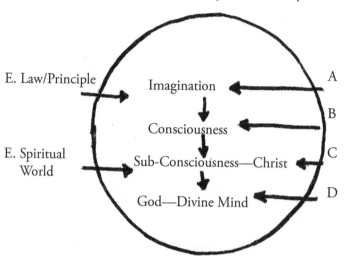

1. Intuition
2. Suggestion
3. Habit
4. Decision
5. Belief
6. Faith
7. Rhythm of thought
8. Your word
9. Dreams
10. Your mind works best:
    a. In quiet and with confidence
    b. When you are calm and relaxed
11. What clogs your mental powers:
    a. Hate
    b. Fear
    c. Negative thinking
    d. Looking backward
    e. Depression
    f. A guilty conscience
    g. Worry
    h. Anger
    i. Sin

Your Imagination

Einstein stated that the imagination is greater than positive knowledge. In your imagination is where all things are created. Make sure you use it for the positive side of life. The imagination sits at the top of your mental powers. Whatever you keep imagining over a period of time activates the subconsciousness or Christ within to help you achieve your goal.

I am going to give you examples from my personal life so you will understand what takes place.

Example 1:

I was in the navy, aboard the USS *Bushnell*. My dad and mother lived on a farm near Afton, Oklahoma. My father had to have an operation and would not be able to ride a tractor for nine months. There was no one to do the farming that summer. I went to the personnel office and told the officer in charge my problem. He gave me a book, listing all of the different types of discharges. As I looked through the book, I came across a "hardship discharge." My intuition (inner feeling) let me know that that was the discharge to request in order to help my family farm.

The officer told me that in twenty years in the navy, he had never seen anyone get out on that discharge. However, he gave me all of the papers to be filled out by a doctor. Each night, I would imagine that I was mowing the front yard at my parents' house, and I could actually smell the fresh-cut grass. I did that every night; and after a while, it seemed real.

When I received the papers, I took them to the personnel office. The officer then sent my application to headquarters. After a short time, I was called to the personnel office, and the officer asked me when I wanted to leave. I had been released from the navy. Through my imagination, I had placed myself on the farm, and it became reality.

Example 2:

By using my imagination, I won an all-expense paid trip to Europe. One of our beauty companies held a contest. Each night, I would get out my Europe program and picture myself visiting each place. I imagined myself cruising from England to France on a boat. After a while, it became so real that I could feel the spray of water on my face as we crossed the English Channel. In the end, my dreams became reality because I dared to imagine the possibility.

Use your imagination on the positive side of life to help you achieve your goals in getting:

1. A wife or husband
2. A house
3. A job
4. A vacation
5. A car, etc.

Get in the habit of writing down your goals and as stated in Proverbs 16:3, "Commit your work to the Lord, and your plan will be established." When you use your imagination to achieve a goal, you also put the law of attraction into motion. Follow your intuition. It will guide you to help you achieve the goal.

The number one mistake that people make is using their imagination on the positive side of life to get wealth, success, and all kinds of material possessions. Then they use their imaginations on the negative side of life on themselves. They begin to say, "I'm getting older," "I have health issues," or "I'm weak." When it comes to yourself, always use your imagination on the positive side of life if you want a positive result.

Your Conscious Mind

Your conscious mind is your watchdog. It is also the captain of your subconscious—Christ within to protect you from anything you do not want to experience in your life. Choose only good and positive ideas to reach your subconscious. For example, be aware of the following:

1. The type of music you listen to

2. The kinds of movies you watch
3. The types of friends you have
4. The kinds of television shows you watch
5. The types of books you read

> Keep thy heart [subconscious/Christ] within with all diligence for out of it are the issues of life. (Proverbs 4:23, King James Version)

Your Subconscious/Christ within Mind

Your subconscious (Christ within) is controlled by your conscious mind. The subconscious (Christ within) does not reason. It only accepts what you suggest for it to do and reproduce by compulsion.

Example:

> If you say, "I am strong," you will be.
> If you say, "I am weak," you will be.

Here we are back to the different use of terminology. You may have heard the subconscious described as

a. The inner mind
b. The infinite mind
c. The Christ within
d. The heart

Whatever you call the subconscious (Christ within), the point you want to remember is that it is one of compulsion, controlled by law and principle. Think of your subconscious mind (Christ within) as a field. Whatever thought you plant in, it is going to grow.

Example:

> Positive, I am youthful.
> Negative, I am getting older.

The Bible states, "As a man thinketh in his heart, so is he." Be transformed by renewing your mind. The universe is spiritual. You are spiritual. Operate from the inside out. After this chapter, I will only use the term *Christ within* instead of subconscious mind because that is what the Bible calls it, the Christ or Christ Jesus within you.

God Divine Mind

You live in a sea of spirit. God, the divine mind and intelligence, is in you, through you, and around you. You are connected to God through your subconscious (Christ within) mind. You are connected to divine intelligence that knows all things. God is good, righteous, and positive. Therefore, if you're wise, you will only think good and positive thoughts to stay on the safe side of the law and principle of life.

Law and Principle

The universe and you are controlled by the law and principle of life. It runs through your subconscious (Christ within) mind and connects you to God. If you think positively, you get a positive result. You are working with the law and principle. If you think negatively, you will get a negative result. For example, if you sin, the result is evil. That means you are going against the law and principle. Furthermore, you will have to pay the consequences until you change your thoughts, words, and actions back to the positive.

Spirit World

The world you live in is spiritual and mental, with a negative and positive side, affecting the word you speak. If you think and speak positively, you get a positive result. If you think and speak negatively, you get a negative result.
Example:

Positive, I am youthful.
Negative, I am getting older.

Your Intuition

Your intuition is a God-given power. It is how God speaks to you. It is that inner feeling that will protect and guide you. The intuition knows information that your senses do not. How many times have you done something against your intuition, when you had a feeling you should not but you went ahead only to regret it later? There have been cases where a person had a reservation on an airplane, experienced a very strong feeling not to fly that day, and the plane went down. The intuition will help you when you are looking for a house, car, or even a spouse. You must learn to follow its directions.

Suggestion

You are using suggestion and repetition when you talk. That is how a habit is formed. The good news is that you can change a bad habit and replace it with a good one. You can think only one word at a time.

For example, each time you make the statement, "I am youthful," you leave an impression in the subconscious (Christ within) mind. After seven to ten days, that suggestion will, through repetition, start to become a habit. Between fifteen and twenty days, it will have become a habit.

The same thing is true if you think negatively. If you keep telling yourself, "I'm getting older," within seven to ten days, that starts to become a habit; and in another five to ten, you will have formed a negative habit. The question is, which way do you want to think, talk, and act? There is great news. You can change any negative habit with a positive statement, the law and principle of life. Remember you are spiritual, and the King James Bible states in Psalm 103:5, "Thy youth is renewed like that of the eagle."

I am youthful.

There is a principle of youth; and the only way you can experience it, to be "renewed like that of the eagle," is to tell yourself that statement every time you think about your age or anyone else's. See the principle of youth in everyone. Whatever you believe in, continue to repeat. Positive: I am youthful. Negative: I am getting older.

The Power of Decision

I have observed many people over the years who had a problem making a simple decision in their daily lives, and they had an even harder time making a decision about a major desire or problem.

I have found there are two reasons people have trouble making decisions. One, they are afraid. They want to please everyone. That is impossible. For example, I am a hairstylist. I have had clients get a frosting in the morning and color their hair back to its natural color in the afternoon because their friends or family didn't give 100 percent approval. To solve that problem, I would tell the client she was going to meet ten people, friends and family, and that half were going to like the frosting while five people wouldn't. Then I would ask if she still wanted the frosting. If the answer was yes, then I frosted her hair. That solved my problem. When making a decision, don't try to please everyone. As long as you aren't violating someone else's rights, follow your own intuition.

Reason two: People have a problem making a decision because they have not done enough research to make a sound decision. Get in the habit of writing out your problem on a paper. Put down everything you can think of that is related to the problem.

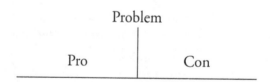

When you are seeking information, only ask people who may have knowledge that will help you solve your problem. Sometimes friends and family are not your best sources for information because they may have an interest that will affect their advice. You should never ask what they would do. Only ask for information that will help you make a wise decision because you are the one who is going to feel the consequences of your choices.

For example, one day I had a patron come into the salon. I will call her Alice. Alice said that a friend had advised her to see me not only to style her hair but to also help her with a problem. Alice, who lived in St. Louis, Missouri, and her late husband Bill had been very close friends with their neighbors, Bob and Rose. Each family bought their houses at about the same time, and both had raised four children, who were grown and married. First, Alice's husband died, and then Bob's wife died. Alice said that after a few years, she and Bob started dating. Finally after some time, Bob suggested that if they got married, they should sell both houses and buy a new one just for them. That is when the problem started.

Alice's four children and half of her family and friends opposed her getting married. Bob had the same issue. His four children and many of his friends and family also opposed the marriage. By the time Alice arrived in Clearwater, Florida, where I was working, she was very confused, and she wanted to know what she should do. I told her that I had come across this problem several times over the years. I told her that I would give her three examples, explaining what had happened in each case, encouraging her to do what she wanted.

After I explained what I had witnessed, I then asked Alice how old she was. Alice said she was sixty. I explained to her that women live, on the average, more than eighty years, and twenty years alone was a very long time. Alice thanked me and said she had something to think about.

About three months later, Alice came waltzing in through the salon doors with her left hand extended. On her ring finger was a three-carat diamond. She and Bob were in Florida on their honeymoon. I asked Alice what had happened. She said she went back to St. Louis and called Bob, inviting him to lunch. She told him what I had explained to her. The next Sunday, Alice invited all of her children for dinner, and Bob did likewise with his family. After dinner, as everyone was sitting in the living room, Alice asked everyone why they were opposed to her getting married. She warned them that she wanted the truth. Their answer was that because they had been brought up in her house, they felt they could come and go as they wished. If she got married, sold the family home, and moved into a new house, they would have to knock on the door when they visited!

Just like Alice, when you are trying to solve a problem, you may have to travel to meet a person for your answer. You might be able to read a book or find the solution in a dream. Keep in mind when you make a decision, you bring into play the power of the universe to work for you. If you make the decision, you can live with it; but if someone else makes the decision, you may never be happy with it. Make sure the decision is on the positive side of life.

Belief and Faith

You have a belief system you use every day. Many of your beliefs about yourself and life were formed when you were very young, and they may be based on the truth. But they may also be based upon what you have been told or heard from family, friends, and society. It would be wise for you to analyze yourself and ask what you believe about the following:

- Your eyes
- Your hearing
- Your youth
- Your age
- Your strength
- Your success
- Your life
- The world you live in

Live your life with faith, belief, and repetitive affirmation. The end result will make a difference in all of your experiences. That is the law and principle of life.

Now faith is the substance of things hoped for,
the evidence of things not seen. (Hebrews 11:1,
King James Version)

So shall my word be that goes forth from
my mouth: It shall not return to me void: But it
shall accomplish what I please and it shall prosper
in the thing for which I send it. (Isaiah 55:11)

So then faith comes by hearing and hearing
by the Word of God. (Romans 10:17)

By faith, start telling yourself that "thy youth is renewed like
that of the eagle." That is what God says about you. By faith, belief,
and repetition, it becomes a habit, and that is how you will start
feeling and acting as if age is not an issue (I am eighty-two, and I
am speaking from experience). Because you are spiritual and operate
from the inside out, God's word is alive. As you go down your check-
list, if you are making a negative statement about yourself or someone else, look through the Bible and replace the negative statement
with positive affirmation. If you are down and depressed, affirm:

The Lord hath made this day, and I will rejoice and be glad in
it. And again!

I am happy, full of joy!

Death and life are in the Power of the tongue,
and those that love it will eat its fruit. (Proverbs
18:21, King James Version)

He who guards his mouth preserves his life.
(Proverbs 13:3, King James Version)

As you can see, the word you speak is creative and has an effect
on your life. Learn to control what you speak and use your mental
power only on the positive side of life.

Your Rhythm of Thinking

You were created with a continual flow of thoughts surging through your mind. Only you can choose which direction you use your word to move toward, the positive or the negative side of life.

Example: Rhythm of Thought

Rhythm of Thought	Positive	I feel good	This is a good day
	Negative	I am getting older	I am tired

When you think that way, you are eating from the tree of good and evil. When you are thinking positively, that is correct; but when you think negatively, that is sin. You are going against the way you and the entire world were created to function. You need to learn to control your thoughts and keep them on the positive side of life.

When forming a new habit, one of the easy ways is to get a notebook so you can write out your affirmations four or five times each night. Then say them out loud.

Example:

"I am happy. I am full of joy."

Express these positive ideas until it becomes a habit. To stay positive is not easy because most people are negative mainly because they are struggling against the way they were meant to use their mental powers. One of the best ways I have found to stay positive is to surround myself with self-help books. I have listed many of them in the back of this book. The Bible should also be your spiritual guide. Each day, read from one of the books to promote a positive attitude. Sadly, you may have to change some friends if they are too negative.

Your Word

The words you speak are a part of your mental process. This process is controlled by law and principle on the subconscious. When you think and speak your word on the positive, good side of life, you are going with the way the universe and your mental powers were created to function. Therefore, you get a positive result. When you speak your words on the negative side of life, sin and evil, you are using your words against yourself and contrary to the way the universe and your mental powers were created to work. Also your words are controlled by law and principle. The words used on the positive side of life have a principle, but words you use on the negative side of life do not have a principle.

Example:

Law	Positive	Life	Love	Youth	Strength
Principle	Negative	Death	Hate	Age	Weakness

So always use your word on the positive side of life. Choose wisely what you speak about yourself and other people.

The law and principle means that by law, when you plant the word *love* (your seed) into your subconscious, Christ within it will start to grow. By principle, the words *love, youth,* and *life* will reproduce after the word of its kind in due time. You cannot think of two words at the same time. Death, life! Which do you choose?

Apply in your life daily

1. "Do not let the Word of Life depart from thy mouth."
2. "I come that they may have life and have it more abundantly."
3. "I am full of life and joy."

These are words in the Bible that have a principle behind them. This will be discussed in more detail in another chapter.

Your Dreams

If you are seeking a solution to a problem, do not overlook your dreams. The answer may come to you in a dream or just after you get up in the morning. I have gotten answers to my problems in dreams. Your subconscious, Christ within, works for you at all times, never sleeping.

Summary:

1. The word you speak is creative and has a positive and a negative side to it.
2. Your imagination is greater than positive knowledge.
3. Your conscious mind instructs your subconscious, Christ within.
4. You live in a sea of spirit and divine intelligence.
5. You are controlled by law and principle.
6. You are guided by your intuition.
7. Your mental powers are working for or against you, twenty-four hours a day, seven days a week.
8. Learn to follow your intuition. It knows things that your common sense does not know.
9. You are controlled by faith, belief, and habit, which you can change.
10. To help keep yourself positive, surround yourself with self-help books and the Bible.
11. Always make positive affirmations about yourself and other people.
12. Do your research before making a decision.
13. A good self-help book can be your best friend.
14. Apply different Bible verses in your daily life. (Example, "The Lord hath made this day and I will rejoice and be glad in it.")
15. You can only think one word at a time (example, positive, love, negative, hate).

Jesus Christ
Your Lord and Savior

The universe you live in is spiritual and mental, with a positive and negative side to it. It is controlled by law and principle that affects your Christ within. Jesus Christ came to show the people (and you) that they were thinking, talking, and acting negatively, contrary to the way their mental powers were created to function.

Adam introduced sin and evil (wrong thinking, talking, and action) which allowed death into the world and cut man off from the mental tree of life. Jesus was born to overcome death. He also can help you regenerate your life and body, promising eternal life to the people and forgiving their sins.

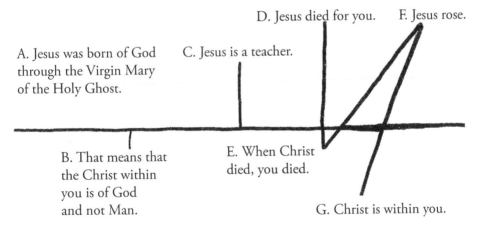

A. Jesus was born of God through the Virgin Mary of the Holy Ghost.

B. That means that the Christ within you is of God and not Man.

C. Jesus is a teacher.

D. Jesus died for you.

E. When Christ died, you died.

F. Jesus rose.

G. Christ is within you.

A. Jesus was born of the Holy Spirit through the Virgin Mary. Jesus tried to teach the people about the spiritual world they live in and their relationship with God, your Father. He came to forgive sins, to help regenerate your life and body, and to overcome death by introducing eternal life to everyone who will follow his teachings. Jesus did not come to prepare you for death but rather for life. There are those who believe because they have accepted Jesus Christ as their Lord and Savior. They are going to heaven. That is what the Bible states. But that is only the beginning. Jesus Christ came to lead you into eternal life, and you have to do your part to achieve this goal. Your work is just starting.

B.   This is to show you that Christ Jesus within you is born of God, the Holy Spirit, and not of man.

Examine yourselves, to see whether you are holding to your faith. Test yourselves. Do you not realize that Jesus Christ is in you? (2 Corinthians 13:5, Revised Standard Version)
   I can do all things through Christ who strengthens me. (Philippians 4:13, King James Version)

C.   Jesus walked among the people, trying to show them the power of Christ within themselves, the power of the spoken word and forgiveness of sins. He led them into righteousness—positive thinking, talking, and acting. Because the people were thinking in negative, sinful ways, they were going against the way the world, and they were created to function. Today when you read the Bible, apply the information to your life. Jesus, your teacher, is teaching you the truth about the spiritual world and your mental powers. Therefore, you are to keep Jesus's sayings and commandments to help lead you through righteousness to eternal life, through Jesus Christ our Lord, here and now, not in the by and by as some teacher.

D. and

E. Jesus Christ died on the cross for your sins. Do you not know that all of us who have been baptized into Christ Jesus were buried into his death so that as Christ was raised from the dead by the glory of the Father, we too might walk in newness of life? For we know that Christ being raised from the dead will never die again. Death no longer has dominion over Him. The death he died to sin (negative thought, talk, action) once and for all, but the life He lives. He lives to God. Therefore, you must consider yourself dead to sin and alive to God in Christ Jesus. Keep in mind you are spiritual and operate from the inside out so that as sin reigned in death, grace also might reign through righteousness (positive thinking, talking, and acting) to eternal life through Jesus Christ our Lord (within you). Now it is time for you to do your part in changing your thinking from negative to positive, thinking about all people and yourself.

And do not be conformed to this world, but be transformed by the renewing of your mind, that you may prove what is that good and acceptable and perfect will of God. (Romans 12:2, King James Version)

There is therefore now no condemnation to those who are Christ Jesus, who do not walk according to the flesh but according to the Spirit.

For the law of the Spirit of life in Christ Jesus has made me free from the law of sin and death. (Romans 8:1–2, King James Version)

Do you not know that you are the temple of God and that the Spirit of God dwells in you? (1 Corinthians 3:16, King James Version)

Therefore, if anyone is in Christ, he is a new creation: old things have passed away; behold, all things have become new. (2 Corinthians 5:17, King James Version)

For if by the one man's offense death reigned through the one, much more those who receive abundance of grace and of the gift of righteousness will reign in life through the one Jesus Christ. (Romans 5:17, King James Version)

F. Thus it is written, and thus it behooved Christ to suffer and to rise from the dead the third day. And that repentance and remission of sins should be preached in his name, among all nations, beginning at Jerusalem (Luke 24:46-47, King James Version).

G. Jesus spake, all power is given unto me in heaven and in earth (Mark 28-18, King James Version).

Now you have to do your part and read the Bible, applying the scripture in your daily life. No one can do it for you!

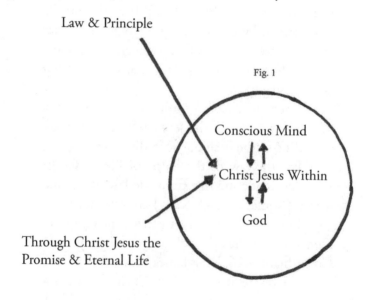

Law & Principle

Fig. 1

Conscious Mind

Christ Jesus Within

God

Through Christ Jesus the Promise & Eternal Life

Christ Jesus within you is your Lord and Savior now.

For we know that Christ Jesus being raised from the dead will never die again: death no longer has dominion over him. The death he died he died to sin, once: But in that he liveth, he liveth unto God. So you also must consider yourself died to sin and alive to God in Christ Jesus. (Romans 6:9–11, King James Version)

But if Christ is in you, although your bodies are dead because of sin, your spirits are alive because of righteousness. If the Spirit of him who raised Jesus from the dead dwells in you, he who raised Christ Jesus from the Dead will give life to your mortal bodies, also through his Spirit which dwells in you. (Romans 8:10, Revised Standard Version)

Do you not know that you are God's temple, and that God's Spirit dwells in you? If anyone destroys God's temple, God will destroy him. For God's temple is holy and that temple you are. (1 Corinthians 3:16–17, Revised Standard Version)

For the love of Christ controls us, because we are convinced that one has died for all; therefore all have died, and he died for all, that those who live might live no longer for themselves but for him who for their sake died and was raised. Therefore, if anyone is in Christ, he is a new creation; the old has passed away, behold the new has come. All this is from God, who through Christ reconciled us to himself and gave us the ministry of reconciliation. (2 Corinthians 14:15, Revised Standard Version)

And this is the testimony that God gave us eternal life, is in his son. He who has not the son of God has not life. I write this to you who believe in the name of the son of God, that you know that you have eternal life. (1 John 5:11–13, Revised Standard Version)

Whosoever shall confess that Jesus is the Son of God, God dwelleth in him, and he in God. So we know one believes the love God has for us. God is love and he who abide in love abide in God, and God abide in him. (John 4:15–16, Revised Standard Version)

For God hath not given us the spirit of fear, but of Power, and of love and of a sound mind. Be not thou therefore ashamed of the testimony of our Lord, nor of me his Prisoner; but be tho partaken of the affliction of the gospel according to the Power of God, Who hath saved us, and called us with an holy calling, not according to our work, but according to His own purpose and grace; Which was given us in Christ Jesus before the World began. But is now made manifest by appearing of our Savior Jesus Christ, who hath abolished death and hath brought life and immortality to light through the gospel. (2 Timothy 1:7–10, King James Version)

God has done His part, and Jesus Christ has done His part. I want to remind you that you are spiritual, and you are a part of the spiritual world. Now it is your time to start removing every negative issue out of your life—negative thinking, negative talking, negative action. Read the Scriptures and apply the information to your daily life. Imitate Jesus Christ and keep his sayings and the commandments. Jesus Christ will lead you to a good, righteous, and positive way of life. That is how the spiritual world and your mental powers were created, to function only on the positive side of life!

Affirmations to use in your daily life:

Therefore, if anyone is in Christ, he is a new creation, old things have passed away; Behold, all things have become new. (2 Corinthians 5:17, King James Version)

But the fruit of the Spirit is love, joy, peace, longsuffering, kindness, goodness, faithfulness, gentleness, self-control. Against such there is no law. (Galatians 5:22–23, King James Version)

If we confess our sins, he is faithful and just to forgive us our sins and to cleanse us from all unrighteousness. (John 1:9, King James Version)

Jesus Christ is the same yesterday, today, and forever. (Hebrews 13:8, King James Version)

Before I formed you in the womb I knew you; Before you were born I sanctified you: I ordained you a prophet to the nations. (Jeremiah 1: 4–5, King James Version)

For God has not given us a spirit of fear, but of power and love and a sound mind. (Timothy 1:7, King James Version)

Do you not know that you are the temple of God and that the Spirit of God dwells in you? (Corinthians 3:16, King James Version)

For the love of the Spirit of life in Christ Jesus has made me free from the low of sin and death. (Romans 8:1–2, King James Version)

And those who are Christ's have crucified the flesh with its passions and desires. If we live in the Spirit, let us also walk in the Spirit. (Galatians 5:24–25, King James Version)

I can do all things through Christ which strengtheneth me. (Philippians 4:13, King James Version)

The Spirit that raised Jesus from the dead dwells in me, and I am being made alive by the same Spirit. (Romans 8:11, King James Version)

Jesus is my Lord and he is my wisdom, righteousness, sanctification, and redemption. (1 Corinthians 1:3, King James Version)

Points to remember:

1. Jesus Christ was born of God, not man.
2. The Christ Jesus within you is born of God.
3. Jesus Christ is your teacher and Savior.
4. When Jesus Christ died, he died for everyone, including you. Now you are alive to God in Christ Jesus.
5. Jesus Christ overcame death, and you are supposed to work to overcome death by following Jesus Christ.
6. All power has been given to Christ Jesus within you.
7. You are to keep Jesus Christ's sayings and commandments.
8. Jesus Christ introduced eternal life back into the world.
9. It is through Jesus Christ that your body and life are regenerated.
10. Use your affirmation in your daily life where it applies.

You Must Forgive Everyone Before You Are Forgiven

There is a cosmic law: you must forgive everyone before you are forgiven. Take this statement very seriously because it can have a major impact on your health and life. I have seen many cases over the years where people have said they would never forgive someone. All they are doing is pumping poison into their bodies, and someday they will have health issues. Hate, resentment, and prejudice—all have to go if you ever hope to feel free, happy, joyful, and healthy.

This is how my journey of seeking the truth began. I had a personal problem that I didn't handle very well, and I allowed hate and resentment to grow to the point that just thinking about that other person or the problem would cause my heart to palpitate. That is when I realized that I had to forgive the other person or destroy myself. My hate habit was so deeply ingrained in my mental powers that just saying, "I forgive ——," didn't solve the problem.

I started to study the Bible, as well as all of the self-help and metaphysical books I could find to solve my problem. Over a period of time, I came up with a formula that worked for me and will work for anyone. Because you are spiritual, if you will apply the information and stay with it as long as it takes, you can overcome your problem.

"Jesus said: I do not say to you seven times, but seventy times seven" (Matthew 18:22, Revised Standard Version) That is 490 times! In other words, to forgive the other person or situation, keep going through the same routine until your conscience is clear and all ill feeling is gone.

There are different methods of forgiveness. The method here is for someone who has a deeply rooted hate that he or she wants to overcome. This is for the person who wants to rid him or herself of hate or depression and begin a renewed life. To overcome your problem, you must stop talking about it to anyone. When you talk about your problem, you are giving it power in your mental power, and that is what you are trying to get rid of.

A. Each night after you get into bed, state,

> Our Father, which art in heaven, I fully forgive [name of person], and I ask that you will forgive me my sins and trespasses. I fully forgive myself in Jesus Christ's name.

B. Then affirm:

> I forget those things which are behind, and I reach forward to those things which are ahead. I press toward the goal for the prize of upward call of God in Christ Jesus. (Philippians 3:13–14, King James Version)

C. Each morning start your day with the following affirmation:

> This is the day which the Lord hath made; I will rejoice and be glad in it. (Psalm 18:24, King James Version)

> Also add, "I am happy and full of joy." Repeat this four or five times.

D. If that person's name should come across your mind, just bless that person and say, "I pray that [name of person] is healthy, wealthy, and happy." Any other statement can be used as long as it is positive. Whatever you are thinking about the other person, you are building in your own mental power first, so you only want something that is good.

After sixty-two days, I awoke one morning, feeling like a new person. All hate and depression were gone. That is why you have to stay with the forgiveness until you feel free. While you are in the process of renewing your mind, you need to remove any fear you may have.

Removing Fear and Worry

When fear, worry, and stress are working in your mental powers, it becomes harder to make a decision, and it can also cause health issues. One thing you must do is take control of your thinking and keep it on the positive side of life. If you are the type of person who is always worrying and fearing what is happening in the world, get out of trying to save the world. God will take care of that. What you need to do is to work on your own mental powers to overcome fear, worry, and stress.

Affirmation:

> For God hath not given us the spirit of fear; but of power, and of love and of a sound mind. (Timothy 1:7, King James Version)
> There is no fear in love; but perfect love casteth out fear; because fear hath torment. He that feareth is not made perfect in love. (1 John 4:18, King James Version)

There is a principle of love but none of fear. Stop thinking about fear and only think of divine love. Take a little time each day, get quiet, and just imagine. Starting at your head, let divine love flow through every atom of your body. Let it flow from you to everyone and everything. After a while, you will discover that love will become a habit, and fear will disappear.

Affirmation:

God is love, and he who abides in love abides in God and God abides in him. (1 John 4:16, King James Version)

Affirmation:

I am calm, cool, and collected. I am afraid of nothing. God is with me.

Use wisdom in your daily life. For example, I live in an area where most of the crime occurs at three different locations at night.

1. The gas station.
2. The 7-Eleven—type stores.
3. The ATM machines.

I am not afraid to go to these places, but I don't go at night. That is not being afraid; that is using wisdom.

Worry

Let me remind you that you are spiritual, and the Bible is your spiritual guide. You were not put on earth without instruction. The Bible is the greatest book on psychology that has ever been written. The information is about the spiritual world you live in but also about your mental powers. If you follow its instructions and move your thinking over to the positive side of life, you may find your worry and fear will disappear.

The law of attraction will work for or against you. That is why you should set a goal to get rid of worry and fear. Reading different books and the Bible will help remove your worry and fear. Why worry about things you cannot change? Will worrying about the price of food, gas, housing, or school help?

There are some salesmen who use fear when trying to sell a house. Between 2004 and 2008, over six million people bought houses they could not afford because they feared if they didn't, they would never find a home. After the financial collapse, they found their house prices upside down. The same thing is happening again in my area. Do not do anything based on emotion or fear. It will usually come out wrong if you do. Make a decision with a cool, calm mind. One of the wise ways to control worry is to live one day at a time, in the "now." Act as if today is all of the time you will ever have.

A. Past	B. Now	C. Future

Past

A. The past is gone. You can never bring it back, so don't waste your energy trying to drag the past with you.
    Affirmation:

I forget those things which are behind and I reach forward to those things which are ahead; I press toward the goal for the prize of the upward call of God in Christ Jesus. (Philippians 3:13–14, King James Version)

If you have lost a loved one, the scriptures say, "Whatever you lose in heaven [your conscious mind] is lost on earth, and whatever you loose on earth is loosed in heaven" (Matthew 18:18). Say I lose (name of person) back to God. Because that person was spiritual and a child of God, when you think of him or her, just bless them and see them as being with God. I have worked with the public for fifty-six years, and I have seen my share of the living dead. They were alive, but they stopped living or going forward when they lost a loved one. They did not release their loved ones back to God and move forward again. Life is always forward; it waits for no one.

Present

B.   The present is all you will ever have. If you learn to live one day at a time, you will be able to solve many of your problems and stop worrying. This is an important point to remember. God within you only operates in the "now," today. Always ask yourself this question: What can I do now, this day, that will make my future a better day? Only what you think now will be reflected in your future, and only you can control what you are thinking, talking, and doing. Stay on the positive side of life today. Don't let the past drain your energy and joy. Also, don't try to live in the future before it gets here.

Future

C.   Now if you have to make a doctor's appointment or plan a trip for some time in the future, you are going to need to do it now. In general, however, God works through your mental power now, today, and can only help you in the "now." You cannot live in the "tomorrow" until it gets here.

Here are some suggestions that I use and suggest to some people to help control worry:

1.   It is said that 90 percent of what you worry about never happens. If you check your past, you will find that to be true.

2.   The pressure method: when you start to worry, put your head against the wall and see how far you get! It is a waste of energy.

3.   Rocking chair method: when you start to worry, sit in a rocking chair and see how far you get. I had a customer who was told by her doctor that if she didn't stop worrying about her grown children, she was going to have a heart attack. I told her about the rocking chair method. When

56

she went home, while sitting in her rocking chair, she started to worry as usual. When she remembered what I had told her, she started to laugh. She said now, every time she sits in that chair, she starts to laugh instead of worrying.

4. Don't cross any bridges until you get there. It is a waste of time to worry about something that has not happened!

Affirmation:

> Thy will keep him in perfect peace whose mind is stayed on thee (God). (Isaiah 26:3, King James Version)

God cannot be described, but we can study the different aspects of God. This is only a small list that you can incorporate into your life:

1. Life
2. Love
3. Truth
4. Divine intelligence
5. Spirit
6. Soul
7. Principle
8. Power

Think over these aspects every day, and they will become a part of your life.

Affirmation:

> Have I not commanded you? Be strong and of good courage; do not be afraid, nor be dismayed for the Lord your God is with you wherever you go. (Joshua 1:9, King James Version)

Worrying is a negative mental habit. Change your thinking to the positive side of life, and you will start to control your worry and your fear.

Points to remember:

1. Forgiveness is a cosmic law, and you must forgive the other person before you are forgiven.
2. Forgive the other person as many times as it takes to clear your mind.
3. Forget the past; only live in the now, today.
4. Give your lost loved one back to God.
5. Worry is a negative mental habit that you need to change to the positive.
6. Do not try to live in the future. God can only help you in the "now," today.
7. Study the different aspects of God. They will become a part of your life.
8. Learn to think on the positive side of life. It will help you conquer your worry and fear.

You Must Be Born Again in Spirit and Truth

Jesus Christ said that you must be born again in spirit and truth.

> He that findeth his life shall lose it; and he that loseth his life for my sake shall find it. (Matthew 10:39, King James Version)

Because the universe is spiritual, you are spiritual, and the word you speak is spiritual and creative. In today's society, it is easy to go against the way the universe and you were created to function. Also you could be going against the law and principle of life.

Therefore, one of the best ways to find life is to give your life to God and accept Jesus Christ as your Lord and Savior. Read the Bible and follow its instructions. Remove all negative thinking, talk, and action. Follow Jesus Christ's sayings, and He will lead you into righteousness and positivity. You will find a newness of life. In fact, you will find life.

The universe has a positive and a negative side to it. The Bible is truth, and the word you speak is spirit. The verse of the Bible is truth. You are to think, talk, and act in a positive manner now.

Example:

- I am strong.
- I am full of life.
- I am full of joy.
- I am youthful.

The problem is that most people do not realize that the universe is spiritual and mental. Neither do they understand that they are spiritual and a part of the universe. They don't know that the word they speak is creative and controlled by law and principle.

Carnal Mind

The carnal mind is one that is not involved in spiritual things. Carnal minds place their faith in the flesh, body, and material things.

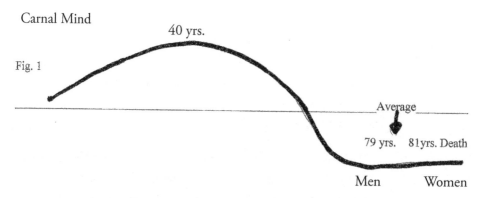

Carnal Mind

40 yrs.

Fig. 1

Average

79 yrs.   81yrs. Death

Men   Women

A person with a carnal mind believes he is born of his parents and lives in a material world only. Each day, he believes that his body is getting older. Saying, "I am getting older," makes it so. He believes he is middle-aged at forty years old. He also might pick up some of these beliefs from family, friends, and society. He has no way to regenerate his body or life; therefore, he becomes ill, grows old, and dies because he never became a part of the spiritual world he lives in. This is why you have to be born again in Spirit and Truth.

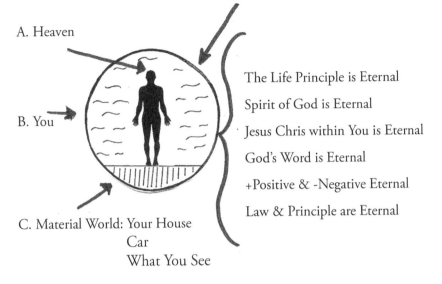

Invisible Spiritual World

A. Heaven

B. You

The Life Principle is Eternal

Spirit of God is Eternal

Jesus Chris within You is Eternal

God's Word is Eternal

+Positive & -Negative Eternal

Law & Principle are Eternal

C. Material World: Your House
Car
What You See

Fig. 2

And do not be conformed to this world, but be transformed by renewing your mind that you may prove what it is that good and acceptable and perfect will of God. (Romans 12:1–2, King James Version)

Affirmation:

As a man thinketh in his heart, so is he. (Proverbs 23:7, King James Version)

Affirmation:

Be transformed by renewing your mind. You live in God's world. It is invisible, spiritual, and mental. It is positive, being governed by law and principle.

A. The Spirit of God is in you, around you, and through you. You have a physical body and a spiritual body and a soul. You are in the middle. On one side, you have the invisible spiritual world; and on the other side is the material world, what you see—your car, house, people, and so forth. Your connection between the spiritual and material world is through your conscience mind.

God can only do for you what He can do through you. Put your index finger on your head and read the following: "Our Father which art in heaven, hallowed be thy name. Thy kingdom come, Thy will be done on earth as it is in Heaven."

Affirmation:

Do not lay up for yourself treasures on earth, where moth and rust consume and where thieves break in and steal. But lay up for yourself treasure in heaven, where neither moth nor rust consume and where thieves cannot steal. For where your treasure is, there will your heart be also.

B. The material world you live in is a reflection of your thinking. If you don't like what you see, change your thinking to the positive side of life, and your world will also change.

C. You live in a spiritual world where the life principle is eternal, and the spirit of God is eternal. Jesus Christ within you is eternal. God's word is eternal.

There is a positive (+) and negative (-). Only think on the positive side of life. It is eternal. The law and principle is eternal. There is only eternal life now.

Spiritual Person

Fig. 3

You Are Born of God_____No end

You are a spiritual person, born of God, through your parents. You have a spiritual body (your soul) and a physical body. You operate from the inside out. Through Jesus Christ, your body is in perpetual regeneration, and the eternal spirit is flowing through you now. Affirmation:

> Be transformed by renewing your mind. (Romans 12:2, King James Version)
>
> As a man thinketh in his heart, so is he. (Proverbs 23:7, King James Version)
>
> Therefore if anyone is in Christ, he is a new creation; old things have passed away; behold, all things have become new. (Corinthians 5:17, King James Version)
>
> For the law of the Spirit of Life in Christ Jesus has made me free from the law of sin and death [Wrong thinking]. (Romans 8:1–2, King James Version)

You must read the Bible yourself if you are going to understand and apply truth in your life._"The holy spirit will teach you" (Luke 12:12, King James Version).

I have known people who have gone to church all their lives and have never read the Bible. My question to you is, if you don't read the Bible yourself, how are you going to know what is right and wrong for you? Many of the things society has accepted as all right are not accepted by God. Truth does not change. Societies do.

To Be Born Again in Spirit and Truth

The word you speak is spirit, and the Scripture is truth. This is where you have to go to work. No one can do your thinking for you! You have to apply the Scripture to reap its benefits. Remove all negative thinking. Keep Jesus Christ's sayings, and He will lead you into righteousness—positive thinking and action.

> For the word of God is living and active, sharper than any two-edged sword, piercing to the division of soul and spirit, of joints and marrow, and discerning the thoughts and intentions of the heart. (Hebrews 4:12, Revised Standard Version)

Do be reborn.
Example:

1. Do not let the word of life depart from my mouth.
2. I am strong.
3. I can do all things with Christ, who strengthens me.
4. I am happy and full of joy.
5. "I am come that they may have life and have it more abundantly" (John 10:10, King James Version).
6. Through Christ Jesus, I see clearly and perfectly, even as the Father in heaven is perfect. I have perfect eyesight.
7. "If any man be in Christ, he is a new creation. Old things have passed away, and all things have become new" (2 Corinthians 5:17, King James Version).
8. "The Lord hath made this day, and I will rejoice and be glad in it" (Psalm 118:24, King James Version).
9. "The Fear of the Lord [law] leads to life and he that has it rests satisfied; he will not be visited by harm" (Proverbs 19:23, King James Version)
10. "Let his [my] flesh become fresh with youth; let him return to the days of his youthful vigor" (Job 33:25, King James Version).

11. "Who satisfieth thy mouth with good things; so that thy youth is renewed like the eagle's" (Psalm 103:5, King James Version).
12. "The fear of the Lord (Law) is the beginning of Knowledge" (Proverbs 1:7, King James Version)
13. "I am the Resurrection and the Life. He that believe in me, though he dies, he will live, and he that live and believes in me will never die" (John 11:25, King James Version).
14. I am healthy.
15. "God is love. He that abideth in love abideth in God, and God abideth in him" (1 John 4:16, King James Version)
16. "He that confesses with his mouth that Jesus is Lord and believe in his heart that God has raised him from the Dead will be saved" (Romans 10:9, King James Version).
17. "Love casts out all fear" (1 John 4:18, King James Version).
18. "For the whole law is fulfilled in one word, even in this: Thou shalt love thy neighbor as thyself" (Galatians 5:14, King James Version).

This is just a partial list of affirmations and verses to help get you started in being born again in spirit and truth. Think positively about everyone and everything. If you can't think of anything positive and good, just bless that person. Follow Jesus Christ, your Lord and Savior. He will lead you into righteousness, into the positive side of life.

Points to remember:

1. You must be born again in spirit and truth.
2. The universe is spiritual and mental, with a positive and a negative side to it.
3. You must be positive. Stop thinking negatively.
4. The Bible is spirit and truth.
5. Jesus Christ within you is your Lord and Savior.
6. If you have a carnal mind, it leads to death.

7. A person with a carnal mind is not connected to the spiritual world.

8. With a carnal mind, you have no way to regenerate your body or life.

9. You are born of God through your parents.

10. You live in an invisible spiritual and mental world that is eternal.

11. Be transformed by renewing your mind.

12. You have a physical and spiritual body with a soul.

13. Your connection between the spiritual world and the material world is through your consciousness.

14. Make the affirmation listed in this chapter a part of your life.

15. The material world you live in is a reflection of your thinking, be it positive or negative.

16. You are a spiritual person.

17. You must read the Bible yourself and apply the verses if you want to regenerate your body and life.

18. You must become one of the doers of the world by applying the verses of the Bible to your life.

19. Your thoughts are things. For example, "I am youthful."

20. Jesus Christ within is your Lord and Savior. Keep His sayings and follow His teachings.

The Mental Tree of Eternal Life
and the Kingdom of God Within

In Chapter 2, we discussed the tree of knowledge of good and evil in the garden of Eden, as well as the tree of life in the middle of the garden. Because of Adam's sin (negative thinking, talking, and acting), man (the human race) was blocked from the tree of life. Adam introduces death into the world.

Jesus Christ, your Lord and Savior, came into the world to overcome death for you, regenerate your body and life. He also introduces eternal life and the kingdom of God within you.

> But if God so clothes the grass of the field, which today is alive and tomorrow is thrown into the oven, will he not much more clothe you, o men of little faith? Therefore, do not be anxious saying, what shall we eat? Or what shall we drink, what shall we wear? For the gentiles seek all these things, and your heavenly Father knows that you need them all, but seek first his kingdom and his righteousness and all these things shall be yours as well. The Kingdom of God is within you through Christ Jesus. (Matthew 6:30–33, King James Version)
>
> With what can we compare the Kingdom of God, or what parable we use for it? It is like a grain of mustard seed, which when sown upon the ground, is the smallest of all the seeds

on earth; yet when it is sown, it grows up and becomes the greatest of all shrubs, and puts forth large branches, so that the birds of the air can make nest in its shade. (Mark 4:30–32, Revised Standard Version)

When you implant God's word, it will produce love in your life.

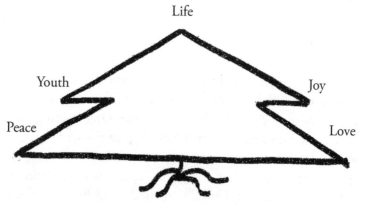

The Kingdom of God within You

Think of each word you apply in your life as a branch. As you add more verses and words from the Bible, your kingdom of God will grow. Each word and verse you implant is your seed, and it will produce after its kind in due time.

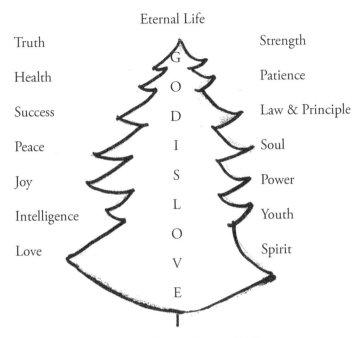

Eternal Life

Truth	Strength
Health	Patience
Success	Law & Principle
Peace	Soul
Joy	Power
Intelligence	Youth
Love	Spirit

GOD IS LOVE

The Mental Tree of Eternal Life

The Kingdom of God Within through Christ Jesus\

This is a partial list of the different aspects of God and the kingdom within. As you read the Bible and keep adding different verses, the kingdom will keep growing and your life will also change for the better.

The universe has a positive and a negative side to it.

Fig. 3

(+)	Positive: Good, Righteousness, Life
(-)	Negative: Sin, Evil, Death

You will only find God's power on the positive side of life. On the negative side, you can do harm to yourself.

Affirmation:

> But the Fruit of the Spirit is love, joy, peace, patience, kindness, goodness, faithfulness, gentleness, self-control; against such there is no law. (Galatians 5:22–23, King James Version)

Not to him who by the power at work within us is able to do far more abundantly, than all that we ask or think, to him be glory in the church and in Chris Jesus to all generations forever and ever. (Ephesians 3:20–21, King James Version)

Each of God's words on the tree of life has a principle behind it. The principle of eternal life is eternal now. Only think of life.

Affirmation:

> Do not let the word of life depart from your mouth.

Affirmation:

> I am come that they may have life and have it more abundantly. (John 10:10, King James Version)
>
> I am the resurrection and life. They that believe in me though he dies, he will live and he that liveth and believe in me shall never die. Believest thou this you are become doers of the word if you are to please God. (John 11:25–26, King James Version)

When you apply the different affirmations in this book, you become a doer of the Word.

Affirmation:

- I am spiritual.
- I am youthful.
- I am full of life.
- I am strong.
- I am happy.
- I am healthy.

You live in God's world. You have to speak what you want into existence before it becomes a reality. Example, I am youthful. Love, peace, and harmony are flowing through every atom of my body. I am strong.

> Death and Life are in the power of the tongue, and they that love it will eat its fruit. (Proverbs 18:21, King James Version)

In a later chapter, I will go into more detail about becoming a doer of the Word.

Points to remember:

1. The kingdom of heaven is within you.
2. The eternal-life principle is here now.
3. The kingdom of heaven can be compared to a mustard seed that grows into a large bush.
4. God's word is the seed that you implant in the Christ within.
5. You should read the Bible yourself to seek the verse or word you want to implant in Christ. Only you can do your own thinking.
6. The universe has a positive and negative side. Speak only on the positive.
7. You will find God's power in your life on the positive side of life.

8. God's word is eternal.
9. You become a doer of the Word when you apply the different affirmations. For example, "I am strong," or "I am youthful."
10. Jesus Christ is your Lord and Savior. Keep His sayings and commandments.

The Principle of Male and Female

You were created with a principle of male and female within you which means you are capable of mentally producing something—speaking the word. "So God created man in his own image, in the image of God created him: male and female created He them" (Genesis 1:27, King James Version)

This does not mean men and women because men and women were not created at that time; they were not created until later. If you look around, you will see there is a male and female principle in every living thing.

1. People	Male	and	Female
2. Animals	Male	and	Female
3. Fowl	Male	and	Female
4. Fish	Male	and	Female
5. Plants	Male	and	Female

You have to have the male to impregnate the female to produce an offspring. I want to remind you again the Bible, from the beginning to the last chapter, is talking to you about the different functions of your mind, your relationship with God, and the universe you live in. As you read and study the Bible, you will find that it has different layers of meaning, and you have to discern what is being said.

Affirmation:

I can do all things through Christ who strengthens me. (Philippians 4:13, King James Version)

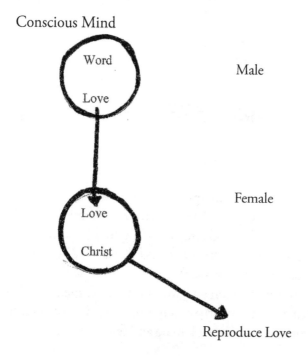

Conscious Mind

Male

Female

Reproduce Love

When you implant the word *love* with your conscious mind (male) into the Christ (female) part of you, you will reproduce what you have said—in this case, love.

As I have already stated, the universe has a positive and a negative side to it. The law runs through you; and if you implant a negative seed or idea into Christ (female), you are going to get a negative result.

> Have ye not read, that he who made them at the beginning made them male and female, And said, For this reason a man shall leave his father and mother and be cleave to his wife: And the twain shall become one flesh? Wherefore they are no more twain, but one flesh. What therefore God hath joined together, let not man put asunder. (Matthew 19:4–6, King James Version)

Now when we look at this verse, there are some very wise advices. If you get married, you are to leave your mother and father and make a life for you and your spouse without interference. This will allow you to do your own thinking and follow your own intuition (God within you). But here again, we are talking about a male and female principle in your mental realm and power.

Fig. 2

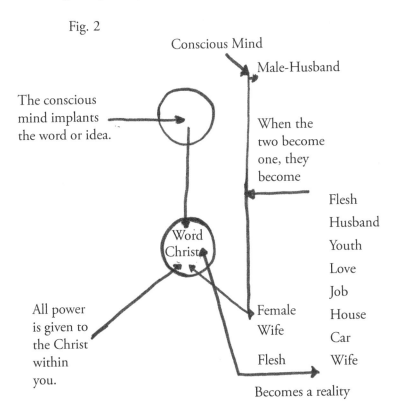

Now if we go back to Genesis 3:20, it reads: "Adam called his wife's name Eve because she was the mother of all living." The Christ within, wife, female part of you, is the mother of all living. When your conscious mind (male) and Christ (female/wife) become one in thought. Example, I am strong. that is going to become flesh in your experience of life. You have already read that a divided house will not stand. It also applies here. If the conscious mind and Christ are not in agreement, your house (life) will not survive. Again I must remind you if you are ever going to learn the truth, you must read and study the Bible yourself to reap its benefits, to regenerate your body and life.

Now you can see why Jesus Christ is your Lord and Savior. All power has been given to Christ Jesus within you. Now Christ is your comforter, helper, regenerator of your body and life, who gives you hope of eternity. You are to keep Jesus Christ, saying the commandments, and following Jesus Christ into righteousness through positive thinking, talking, and acting positively. Remove all negative thoughts, words, and actions from your life. Now. "For he is not a God of the Dead, but of the living for all live unto him" (Luke 20:38, King James Version)

Points to remember:

1. There is a principle of male and female in the universe.
2. There is a mental principle of male and female within you.
3. The conscious mind is referred to as the male, and Christ is referred to as the female because that is where all the power and creative process operates.
4. You use your conscious mind to implant God's word or an idea into the Christ within, and it will reproduce that word or idea in due time. For example, if you implant love, you get love. If you implant "I'm strong," you get youthfulness.
5. If you implant a negative word or idea, you will get a negative result.
6. When you get married, you are to leave your mother and father so God can walk through you.
7. When your conscious mind implants a word or idea into the Christ and the two become one in thought, it becomes flesh, a reality.
8. All power is given to the Christ Jesus within you. Now.
9. You are to follow Jesus Christ by keeping his sayings, the commandments, into righteousness.
10. God is not a god of the dead but of the living.

Through the Eye of a Needle

> It is easier for a camel to go through the eye of nee-
> dle than for a rich man to get into the Kingdom
> of God (Mark 10:25, King James Version)

To get a better understanding of this statement made by Jesus Christ, let's go back to the beginning. The world you live in is spiritual, mental, and material. You are a child of God, born of God. You are spiritual. If God gives you a talent and you develop that skill, whether it be playing ball, writing a book, or working in a professional field, you have developed an idea that God has given you. I don't think God is going to condemn you if that talent or idea brought you millions of dollars. It was, remember, God who gave you the talent or idea in the first place.

Also the scripture states that it is the Lord that giveth you the power to get wealth. I think we can safely say it is not the riches that keep you out of the kingdom of God. The eye of a needle was a small entrance into some ancient city, and the camel had to be unloaded before he could go through the entrance. How much baggage do you need to let go of? Hate, pride, self-centeredness, negative thinking? You need to unload to get into the kingdom of God.

Have you ever given thanks or donated money to support God's kingdom? Or do you think you made the riches on your own? If you believe you made your wealth on your own, you have put your riches before God. You have broken more than one of the commandments. You have made money your god.

Let's analyze what your money will buy you in the material side of life.

1. Money will buy almost any material thing—car, house, clothes, etc.
2. Travel
3. Any type of attraction
4. Sex
5. Negative things, such as drugs and alcohol
6. An education
7. A business
8. Investments
9. All of the comforts of home
10. The ability to give orders to other people
11. Entertainment

All of these things listed are issues of the flesh and the world, many of which can lead you to destruction. These items will not help you get into the kingdom of God. "For what does it profit a man to gain the whole world and forfeit his life? For what can a man give in return for his life" (Mark 8:36, King James Version)?

The Spiritual and Mental World

You live in a spiritual, mental, and material world. Each of the different items listed below are spiritual in nature, and these are what your money cannot buy.

1. Eternal life
2. Renewed life
3. Renewed youth
4. Health
5. Happiness and joy
6. Absence of fear
7. Regeneration of body and life
8. Inner security

9. Rebirth of spirit and truth
10. Forgiveness of sins
11. Absence of hate and resentment
12. The Lord and Savior within you
13. Peace and harmony
14. Love
15. Ability to think
16. Renewed strength
17. The kingdom of God
18. A renewed spirit
19. God

> For the Kingdom of God does not mean food, drink, but righteousness, peace, and joy in the Holy Spirit. (Romans 14:17, Revised Standard Version)
>
> Do not be deceived; God is not mocked for whatever a man sows that he will also reap. For he who sows to his own flesh will from the flesh reap corruption. But he who sows to the Spirit will form the Spirit reap eternal life. (Galatians 6:7–8, Revised Standard Version)

Now you can see what your money will and will not buy. To get into the Kingdom of God, you have to do something else.

> He who finds his life will lose it, and he who loses his life for my sake will find it. (Matthew 10:39, King James Version)
>
> Do not be conformed to this world. But be transformed by the renewing of your mind that you may prove what is the will of God, what is good and acceptable and perfect. (Romans 12:2, King James Version)

The universe is spiritual, mental, and material. The Bible is your spiritual guide to live by.

"Submit yourself therefore to God. Resist the devil and he will flee from you. Draw near to God, and He will draw near to you" (James 4:7–8, King James Version). Accept Jesus Christ within you as your Lord and Savior. He is also your teacher. All the power has been given to the Christ Jesus within you. When you submit your life to God, that means you are going to accept Jesus Christ as your Lord and Savior and align your thinking to the Scriptures. It also means that you are going to look on the positive side of life and remove all sin, negativity, and wrong thinking, talking, and acting from your life. You must also be born again in spirt and truth. That was discussed in Chapter 7.

If you follow Jesus Christ, keep his sayings and commandments, He will lead you into righteousness and positive actions. Remember that the universe has a positive and a negative side. You will find God's power through Jesus Christ if you journey on the positive side of life, the pathway to the kingdom of God.

> For the Word of God is quick and powerful and sharper than any two-edged sword. Piercing even to the dividing asunder of Soul and morrow, and is a discerner of the thoughts and intents of the heart. (Hebrews 4:12, King James Version)

There is also a law and principle that controls your thinking and the words you speak. Example, "Thy youth is renewed like the eagle's" (Psalm 103:5, King James Version).

I am youthful. There is a principle of youth and none of age. In spirit, there is no time, and your age is not a factor. The spirit has control over the flesh; you operate from the inside out. By law, the word *youth* is going to grow within your experience; and by principle, you will have renewed youth in your life. You will feel it in your life and see it in your skin. I am eighty-two years old. I am talking from experience. The word you speak is spirit, and the verses from the Bible are truth. When you read the Bible, take different verses and apply them in your life. Always speak with positivity.

You now have crossed over from the material world into the spiritual and mental world. In the material world, your attitude maybe "I will believe it when I see it!" In the spiritual world, by faith, you have to speak the word, "I am happy and full of joy," until it becomes a reality. You must become a doer of the Word to experience the benefits of the word spoken.

Here are some affirmations to help you to get started on your way to the kingdom of God.

A. I can do all things through Christ, who strengthens me.
B. The word is very near me, in my mouth and in my heart, that I may do it.
C. I am full of life.
D. He is to come that I may have life and have it more abundantly.
E. I am strong.
F. I am youthful.
G. God is love. He that abides in love abides in God, and God abides in him. God abides in me.
H. I am healthy.
I. I see clearly and perfectly as the Father in heaven is perfect.
J. Love, peace, and harmony are flowing through every atom of my body.
K. Do not let the word of life depart from my mouth.
L. Eternal life is flowing through every atom of my body. Now.
M. I am successful.
N. The Lord hath made this day, and I will rejoice and be glad in it.
O. I bless my youthful skin.
P. Jesus Christ is my Lord and Savior within.
Q. I will watch what I allow to enter my mind, letting in only that which I want to experience in my life.

Becoming a doer of the Word will be discussed in more detail in the last chapter of this book.

Points to remember:

1. You are a child of God, born of God.
2. You are a spiritual being living in a spiritual world.
3. It was God who gave you the power to accumulate wealth.
4. Do you have any negative baggage that you need to get rid of?
5. You can't buy your way into the Kingdom of God.
6. Only you can do your own thinking.
7. Your money will not buy anything that is spiritual.
8. You have to change your thinking from negative to positive in order to enter the kingdom of God.
9. You have to accept Jesus Christ within as your Lord and Savior.
10. You must become a doer of the Word.
11. Only you can renew your spirit.
12. The Bible is your spiritual manual to live by.
13. You must read the Bible yourself to reap its benefits.
14. You have to be born again in spirit and truth.
15. Only you can speak the word in your life.
16. The word you speak is controlled by law and principle.
17. Practice your affirmations until they become a habit.
18. In the spiritual world, you have to speak the word first before it becomes a reality in your life experience. For example, "I am happy and full of joy!"

Your Hair, Skin, and Beauty

"Thou shall decree a thing and it shall be established unto you" (Job 22:28, King James Version) You are born of God. You live in a spiritual world; and you are spiritual, with a spiritual body operating from the inside out. The word you speak is creative, having a negative and positive side to it. The word you speak about yourself and others will have a direct effect on your hair, skin, and beauty.

After working in the beauty field for fifty-five years, I have found that there are several major causes of hair loss.

1. Medicine
2. Thyroid
3. Stress
4. Disease
5. Beliefs

Medicine. When a customer starts to complain about hair loss, I ask if he or she is taking any medication. Some medicines cause the hair to thin. In some cases, the medicine can be changed, and that solves the problem. I had a female customer who had a big bald spot on her scalp. She said she had gone to a dermatologist, but he couldn't figure out what was wrong. She was only taking one medicine for her heart, and her cardiologist said the hair loss was not due to the prescription. I told the lady to ask the doctor the next time she saw him if there was any new literature about the medication. When she did, the doctor told her that he had a lot of papers on his desk, but he would look through them and get back with her. Three days later, my client received a call from her doctor. After having the medication on the market for six years, the pharmaceutical company had published information stating that one possible side effect was a bald spot on the scalp. Her doctor changed her prescription, and her hair grew back. I have seen cases in which people lost the hair on the tops of their heads. After their medicines were changed, their hair returned.

Thyroid. If there is an imbalance in a person's thyroid, it can cause hair loss. Your doctor can check your thyroid. In most cases, if there is a thyroid issue and medicine is administered, the hair loss stops. In some instances though, the thyroid medicine itself can cause the problem, and there is nothing that can be done about it. I had a customer who was on thyroid medicine, and her hair kept coming out. She had her thyroid rechecked, and her doctor said that her prescription was the correct one for her. However, her hair kept falling out. I told her to take the prescription bottle to her doctor and have him check the prescription against their records. They found out that the pharmacist had made a mistake. When the prescription was corrected, her hair loss stopped.

Stress. Stress is a major health issue. Stress and worry can cause hair loss. There are many different types of stress caused by family, friends, work, death, and divorce. To remove stress should be one of your major goals. There are many books, including the Bible, which could help you overcome stress if you read them and apply the information in your life.

Disease. In the fifty-five years that I have worked with the public in the salon, I have had only one case in which the doctor said that a customer had a disease of the scalp. She was given a prescription that helped to correct the problem.

Beliefs. You are spiritual. You live in a spiritual and mental world, controlled by law and principle, positive and negative. Your word is alive and creative. When I use the word *beliefs*, I am referring to what you keep suggesting to yourself.

Example:

Positive	I have thick hair.
Negative	My hair is getting thin.

84

Your belief system was formed when you were very young, made up of what your parents, family, and friends said. Most people make a negative statement about their hair or believe they inherited their thin hair from someone else, such as an aunt or some other relative, because their mother told them so when they were small. As long as you believe your hair is thin because you inherited this trait from a family member, your hair will stay that way until you change your mind and believe.

I am living proof of what I am about to say. The Christ in you has the power to put hair on your head or take it off. When I was about forty years old, my hair started to thin. My father and my brother both had hair that had thinned considerably. However, both of my grandfathers had thick hair. I asked myself why my hair was thinning. I realized that I had formed a false belief that with age, a person's hair naturally grew thinner. Throughout our lives, you and I have heard this said by family, friends, doctors, and television advertisers. When I learned about my own mental powers and started suggesting to myself, my hair started to get thicker. Now, at age eighty-two, I have thick, wavy hair. Age is not a factor!

After that, I started asking my clients why they believed that their hair was thinning. Many times, the answer was "my mother told me I inherited my thin hair from my aunt so and so." I have great news for you. You never inherited anything from your aunt so and so unless you believe it.

Example 1: I had a customer in her seventies, and she had thin hair. I asked her why she believed her hair was thin, and she said her mother told her that she had inherited the tendency. I explained how her mental powers functioned, advising her from that day forward to always make a positive statement about her hair, such as telling herself that her hair was getting thicker. I told her to repeat these positive statements while looking in a mirror and to avoid telling anyone because most people will just laugh or make some wisecrack. They do this because they do not understand the law and principle that is at work here. After a year or so, the woman went to visit her son in Dearborn, Michigan. When they met at the airport, he said, "Mom,

I don't know what you're doing, but your hair looks thicker than I have ever seen it." Nothing could have made her happier.

Example 2: A lady I will call Kim was in her fifties, and she came into the salon for a haircut. Kim had a thinning spot about three inches in diameter on the top of her head. The hair around the area was much thicker. I asked Kim why she believed her hair was like this, and she again said that it was inherited. I explained to Kim how her mental powers worked. Over a period of time, after making daily positive statements to herself, Kim's hair grew back.

You are a spiritual being living in a spiritual world. You have to repeat the word first before you see any results. When I tell someone to make a positive statement, such as "I have thick hair," and that person says, "I will try," I tell him or her to forget it. It will not work for that individual because he or she has doubt. Trying is doubting.

Example 3: I knew a young lady in her twenties named Kay. Her hair was about eighteen inches long and thin. I knew her mom and dad, both of whom had thick hair. I asked Kay why she believed her hair was so thin since her parents had thick hair. Once again, Kay said her mother had told her that she had inherited the trait from an aunt. After suggesting that she use her positive mental powers, I watched over time, and the results were wonderful.

Example 4: Another client, whom I will call Rosa, is in her eighties. When she started coming into the salon, her hair was very thin on top, revealing her pick scalp. I explained to her, just as I had to the others, about using her mental powers to overcome this. After she had made positive statements about her hair for a year, it had become much thicker. Her hair is now doing great. When people ask her what she is doing to make her hair thicker, she says that she talks to it, and they just laugh.

Thick Hair

When I was working in Arizona, I had a costumer, Chris, with the thickest hair I have ever worked on in fifty-five years. I asked her why she believed her hair was so thick. Chris said her mother told her she would always have thick hair because she was part Indian; and boy, did Chris have hair! How much was due to her ethnicity and how much was the result of her belief? We'll never know.

If you are a mother with a small child, regardless of what the child's hair looks like, make a positive statement about it. For example, tell the child that he or she is going to have thick hair when he/she grows up. Your children are going to believe what you tell them about their hair. They will grow into the types of customers I have who, even in their eighties and nineties, need to have their hair thinned in order to have it lie correctly.

To show you the strength of your mental power, I would like to tell you about an incident when my wife and I went to a car dealership showroom in El Cajon, California, to look at the new cars. When we entered the show room, two salesmen started to talk to us and to show us the new cars. After a while, one asked me what kind of work I did. I said that I was a hairstylist. There was another salesman whom I will call Don. The first two called Don over to where we were. Don had a bald head. One of the other salesmen rubbed Don's head and asked if I could do anything with his head. I said we might buy him a wig, and we all laughed.

After the other salesmen walked away, I asked Don if he had any brothers and if he did, were they also bald. Don said he had three brothers who, along with their dad, all had full heads of hair. I asked Don why he thought he was bald. He replied that since he was sixteen, he had always wanted to be bald. He had shaved his head until he turned fifty when he did not need to shave anymore. Don had actually become bald. So you can see that you have a power inside you that can put hair on your head or take the hair off your head by your spoken word.

Most of the customers who come into the salon are looking for a hairstyle, a cut, or a product to make their hair thicker. I have to be careful to whom I advise the power of positive suggestion. Most people have their own belief systems about their hair, and I don't want to offend anyone.

Affirmations:

1. I have thick hair.
2. "As a man thinks in his heart, so is he" (Proverbs 23:7, King James Version)
3. "Thou shall decree a thing, and it shall be established unto you" (Job 22:28, King James Version)
4. "Be transformed by renewing your mind" (Romans 12:2, King James Version)
5. "I can do all things Christ who strengthens me" (Philippians 4:13, King James Version)

This truth is about you, so make positive statements about your hair and about the hair of others. Learn these affirmations and verses. Apply them to your daily life.

Your Skin, Beauty, and Life

In the beauty field, we are working with different types of skin problems. I used to work with a stylist whom I will call Diane. Although she was about forty-eight years old, Diane had one of the most beautiful complexions that I have ever seen. I asked Diane what she used on her skin to make it look nearly flawless. Diane said that after washing her face, while the skin was still wet, she always used an inexpensive moisturizing cream on her fact. Then she would take a Kleenex and blot off the excess cream. That was thirty-five years ago. Since that time, I have used that same method. I can say it works great, keeping the skin soft, moist, and flexible.

There are some activities that may cause skin problems, resulting in the need for special care.

Causes of Skin Problems

1. Going to the beach
2. Sunbathing
3. Using tanning beds

4. Golfing
5. Playing tennis
6. Smoking
7. Living on the negative side of life
8. Suffering an illness
9. Consuming too much alcohol
10. Experiencing stress

Beachgoers

If you are the type who loves the beach, you should always use a sunscreen to protect your skin. Watch how long you are exposed to the sun. What you do now to protect your skin will determine what your skin looks like thirty, forty, or fifty years later.

Sun bathers and tanning-bed users

Both should use the same care as beachgoers in protecting your skin

Golfers

I have seen many clients who are golfers. Many times their skin is very dry and wrinkled even though the people are only in their forties, fifties, or sixties. Do everything you can while you are youthful to protect your skin. Use sun screen and wear a hat or visor.

Tennis players

Do the same as golfers.

Smokers

Smoking reduces the oxygen supply to your body and skin. This causes wrinkles and affects the color of your skin. Stop smoking!

Those who live on the negative side of life

You are spiritual; and when you live on the negative side of life, you are going against yourself and the way you were created to function. In some cases, negative people have skin that looks ten years older than they really are. You were created to live on the positive side of life. I have had customers in their eighties, nineties, and up who read the Bible regularly and attended church. Due to these positive influences in their lives, they had very few wrinkles on their faces.

The ill

A long illness will affect anyone's skin. If the ill person recovers, usually the skin will also improve. A man brought his wife into my salon. She had been ill, and he asked if I could give her a perm. He thought it might make her feel better. I said I would make her look ten years younger. After I had cut and permed her hair, her husband agreed that she had indeed lost ten years. The next time she came in, she asked me how old I thought she was. I guessed that she was about forty-five. She said she was only thirty-five. I had put my foot into my mouth, and I was determined to never try to guess a person's age again. Obviously, her illness had prematurely aged her, especially her skin.

Alcohol users

If you drink too much alcohol, you and others will be able to see the effects in the color of your skin. It can cause sallowness, redness, and blotchiness. Of course, alcohol can also affect other parts of your body too.

Those who are stressed

Doctors have found that stress can cause many different types of illnesses and physical problems. Stress can also affect your skin and hair if you do not learn to control it. Make stress relief one of your major goals in life. If you make it a goal, you will be able to find information from books and experts who will help you get a grip on your stress level. Do not get stressed out about things you cannot control or change. The Christ within you knows how to achieve a stress-free life.

Sit down and write all of the different things that are causing you stress in your life. Take one thing at a time, and do what is necessary to remove a particular stressor. That may mean changing some friends, blessing someone, or spending less time with family. To help reduce stress, remember that 90 percent of what you worry about never happens. Don't cross any bridges until you get there. Don't worry about something that hasn't happened yet. The following affirmations will help you to control stress.

1. "A cheerful heart is a good medicine, but a downcast spirit dries up the bones" (Proverbs 17:22, Revised Standard Version)

2. I am happy and full of joy.

3. The Lord hath made this day. I will rejoice and be glad in it.

4. "Let his flesh become fresh with youth; let him return to the days of his youthful rigor" (Job 33: 25, Revised Standard Version)

5. "Thy youth is renewed like the eagle's" (Psalm 103:5, King James Version)

6. I am youthful. I bless my firm, youthful skin.

Let me remind you that you are spiritual and operate from inside out. These affirmations have truth and life in them if you apply them to your daily living. You will start to feel and think differently, and your skin will also respond to what you are saying. You operate from the inside out, and the word you speak is spirit that is controlled by law and principle. The spirit, then, has control over the flesh. "To set the mind on the flesh is death, but to set the mind on Spirit is Life and Peace" (Romans 8:6, Revised Standard Version)

Your Beauty

You are spiritual, born of God through your parents into a spiritual world. You are a child of God, one of a kind. There is no one in the world that looks like you or has your personality. You are unique. You are an individual like no one else. Why do you want to look like everyone else when it comes to your hair, makeup, and clothes? Beauty is more than one's appearance.

Over the years, I have met thousands of people from around the world. Out of all those people, only one person I met thirty-five years ago stands out, and I have never forgotten her. On a Sunday morning, I was walking through our apartment complex where we lived. I was by our tennis courts when a young lady in her mid-twenties came from the other direction. I looked at her and thought to myself that she was not very attractive. As she got closer, she stopped and started to talk to me. She had a very nice smile, and she spoke in a very pleasant voice. As we continued to talk, her appearance began to change, and I looked at her differently. This lady had an extremely positive personality, radiating beauty from the inside out.

Your personality is more important than how your face and hair look. What you carry inside will also reflect in your skin. I have met many women who were beautiful; but when they spoke, they had foul mouths, lax morals, or self-centered tendencies. Physical beauty fades with time. A person with a pleasing smile, a positive mental attitude, and winning personality will reflect beauty.

Always be an individual. Do what makes you feel the most beautiful. Always make positive statements about yourself. Don't let anyone try to change you into something you are not. Stay away from the kind of people who would try to change the real you.

You do not know what was planted in your inner mind when you were a child. Some of these thoughts might have been negative, and you need to overcome them. You are spiritual and a child of God. You have control over what you think and say about yourself. Whatever someone else says about you means nothing unless you believe it. Always make statements to yourself that are positive.

Affirmations:

1. "Thy youth is renewed like the eagle's" (Psalm 103:5, King James Version).
2. I bless my youthful skin.
3. I am happy and full of joy.
4. I feel attractive.
5. I have a pleasant smile.

If you don't talk to yourself, who is? After working with the public for fifty-five years, I am convinced that the best way to improve someone's beauty is to cultivate a pleasant smile along with a positive, kind, and outgoing personality. You must talk positively to yourself in order to obtain these traits. Every time you make the statement, "I am getting older," you are cutting off the flow of life. Remember John 10:10, "I am come that they may have Life and have it more abundantly." There is a law and principle of life. You are spiritual; and in spirit, there is no time. Always speak positively to yourself to build yourself up.

Points to Remember:

1. You are spiritual. Always make positive statements about your hair.
2. Your word that you speak is creative. Always speak positively to yourself.
3. Medicine is the major cause of hair loss.
4. What do you believe about your hair?
5. Make it a goal to remove stress from your life.
6. Always make a positive statement about your hair. Example, "I have thick hair."
7. Age is not a factor when it comes to hair.
8. Belief will put hair on your head or take it off.
9. When you were small, what did your mother tell you about your hair?

10. You have a power within you that can put hair on your head or take the hair off your head.
11. Do what is necessary while you are youthful to protect your skin and beauty.
12. Apply a moisturizing cream on your face while it is still wet.
13. When you apply your affirmations, you are becoming a doer of the Word.
14. The spirit (word) you speak has control over the flesh.
15. Beauty is more than your appearance. Your personality is just as important.
16. Always think life; there is a principle of life.
17. Stop saying, "I am getting older." Affirm, "I am youthful."
18. Always make a positive statement about your child's hair.
19. Talk to yourself positively about your hair, skin, and beauty.
20. You are one of a kind. Do not let anyone try to change you.

Truth and Your Health

You live in a spiritual and mental world. You are spiritual, and the Bible is your personal manual to live by here on earth. Therefore, if you want to enjoy the benefits of the Bible and good health, you must read the text yourself and align your thinking to what the Bible tells you to do, applying the verses to your life.

Health is made up of many components. If you need to go to a doctor, you should go. If you need surgery, you should have it done. You should get your annual checkup. The information here is to help you set some control over your health. This is a preventive approach to health.

There are two parts to your health, spiritual/mental and physical. What you do as a young person will have an effect on your health forty, fifty, or sixty years later. You might know all of these issues, but what are you doing to help yourself to protect your health?

The Physical Side of You

1. Air

You should do everything you can to protect the air you breathe. If your job requires a mask, wear it. There are many work areas where the air is not of the best quality. It might not bother you now; but it might forty, fifty, or sixty years later when it affects your health. Over the years, I have seen plenty of people on oxygen because of contaminants in the air—including spray, paint, and other products. So always try to protect your air supply.

2.   Food

Your body needs certain vitamins and minerals to function properly. The food you eat is going to determine how healthy your body is. We have become a fast-food society. There is nothing wrong with eating fast food every now and then; but if it is your primary diet, you may not get what your body needs. You need vegetables, fruits, nuts, and other foods to have a balanced diet. Your health problems caused by a poor diet might not emerge for thirty, forty, or fifty years.

3.   Exercise

Your body was not made just to sit. You lose your strength by doing nothing. Walking is one of the best exercises you can do to stay fit and maintain a healthy body. Working in the yard is also beneficial to your health. When I work in the yard, I think of it as yard exercise. Your strength is also controlled by what you think.

"I can do all things through Christ who strengthens me" (Philippians 4:13, King James Version). I am strong. These powerful affirmations that you speak to yourself are very powerful. I have seen a lot of people in their forties, fifties, and sixties lose their strength due to a lack of exercise and a negative mental attitude. They blame it on old age.

4.   Smoking

It amazes me that after all of the advertising that shows the effects of smoking, people continue to light up. Smoking affects the oxygen supply to your body, which it needs to function properly. I have seen many people who stopped smoking twenty-five or thirty-five years ago, but the damage was already done to their lungs. Thirty to fifty years later, they are on oxygen, just trying to breathe. In the meantime, smoking has also created other health issues for them. If you are a smoker, you will not stop until you make up your mind to quit. Do you want to be on oxygen for years? Is it worth it to you?

5.   Sleep

Today getting the proper amount of sleep is a major problem for many in our society. Sleep is natural. The question you need to ask yourself is what am I doing wrong? What is keeping you from getting seven to eight hours required sleep to maintain a healthy body and lifestyle? Your sleep is controlled by habit. If you are having trouble, you have allowed your body to take over and to knock you out of your normal sleep habit. I know what it feels like because I have been there, and it took some time to get back into my normal sleep habit, but it was worth all of the effort. It is important that you have a set time to go to bed, perhaps 11:00 p.m., and a set time to get up, such as 7:00 a.m. When you set your timer, that is the goal you are going to work toward; that is your starting point. I have seen people allow their sleep habits to get out of control, causing them to be up all night and asleep most of the day. They then complain about how tired they feel.

The first step is to prepare your bedroom and yourself. Your bedroom is for sleep. Turn off or remove the television. Get rid of all phones. Keep the room cool, approximately seventy-two degrees, so you don't become too warm. I use a small ten-inch fan to block out all outside noise. If you get used to a fan, you won't want to sleep any other way. How late you eat and drink will have an effect on your sleep too. Work to remove all stress and worry, practicing some relaxation exercises prior to bedtime.

I got out of my sleep cycle, and it took some time to get back to my regular schedule, 11:00 p.m. to 6:30 a.m. In order to accomplish this, I made a sleep calendar, so I could see what was helpful and what was distracting me from getting a good night's sleep. You can use the same method to help you get and stay in your regular sleep cycle if you apply this information.

Sleep Calendar

Example: Day

	1	2	3	4	5	6	7 8 9 10 11 12 13 14 15 16 17 18 19 20
Food	✓						
Drink	✓						
TV	X						
Phone	X						
Book	✓						
News	X						
Animals	X						
Noise	✓						
Bed Time	11						
Rising Time	6						
Hours Asleep	7						

The next morning, when you get up, check each item to see what effect it had on your sleep. For example, if what you ate didn't bother you, put a check in that space. If watching television kept you awake, put an X in that box. Then write down the number of hours you slept. Over a period of time, you will notice a pattern forming. Some nights you will get more sleep than others. Stop doing what kept you awake and do the things that help improve your sleep. Due to your work, school, or children, each person has to set his or her own sleep cycle. If you don't have an alarm clock, get one.

I knew a couple in their nineties. The wife had gotten out of her sleep cycle and was up most of the night. Of course, she felt exhausted all day. I asked them if they had an alarm clock. They both laughed, saying they hadn't had an alarm clock for thirty-five years. I told them to buy a clock, which they did. I asked the woman what time she wanted to go to bed and what time she wanted to get up. She said she would like to go to sleep at about midnight and get up at eight each day. I told her to set the alarm for eight and go to bed as usual. The next day, she was to set her alarm for 7:30, moving the time up in thirty-minute increments each day until she started falling asleep earlier due to fatigue. Within a short time, she was back into her sleep cycle.

If you are having trouble sleeping, you should never take a mid-day nap. If you do, you will have even more trouble getting to sleep that night. I have heard people say if you can't sleep, you should get up and watch television or read. I want to point out to you that if you start getting out of bed two or three times a week, you are creating a new habit, and you will start waking up at that time. Is that what you want?

When you get into bed or wake up during the night to use the restroom, when you get back into bed, do not ever start thinking about work or a problem you are having. It will only make you more awake. Bedtime is your peace time. Think of something pleasant, such as a walk on the beach or in a garden. It will help you go back to sleep.

6. Alcohol

Just watch the 5:00 p.m. news each day, and you can see what problems alcohol causes in many lives—car wrecks, murders, divorces, crimes. And that is just the beginning. Too much alcohol can have a negative effect on your body and health.

"No longer drink only water, but use a little wine for the sake of your stomach and your frequent ailments" (Timothy 5:23, King James Version). The point here is you have to decide what purpose alcohol will play in your life. Don't let it destroy your health and life. Develop some new interests in life, and your desire to drink will diminish.

7. Drugs

You may have to use some drugs to help you maintain health. It is very important that you understand why you are taking each drug. I had a customer whose doctor told her she had six months to live, so she and her husband moved back to New Jersey to be near their family. Six months later, I received a call from her. I said, "I thought you went home to die. What happened?"

She said that her family doctor asked her to come in and to bring all of her pills. The doctor set all of the bottles on his desk. The doctor picked one up, asked why she was taking that pill. She said it was for her heart. He then picked up a second bottle and asked why she was taking that pill. She said that she didn't know, so the doctor threw it away. The doctor continued to ask about each pill bottle; and if she couldn't tell him the purpose for the drug, he threw it away. Out of the eight bottles of pills she had been taking, the doctor kept only three. The woman said after three months, she started feeling better, and they moved back to Florida.

This is just once case of many in which a person was taking too many pills that didn't benefit the health of the individual but rather had a negative effect. Know why you are taking any pills that are prescribed to you. Also take them correctly.

8. Illegal drugs

Illegal drugs not only destroy your health but also your life. Think twice before you get involved in these drugs. Get high on life. Develop a new interest or find a way to help someone else.

9. Hate and resentment

Hate and resentment can cause a lot of health issues if you do not get them out of your system. You are to forgive the other person before you are forgiven. This cannot be overstated. Reread Chapter 6.

10. Negative thinking

Negative thoughts, speech, and actions are destructive to your health and can cause all different types of physical issues. When you think negatively, you restrict the flow of life. One common way people do this is by saying, "I am getting older." Remember, negative thinking attracts negative results. That is the law of life.

11. Positive thinking

You are spiritual, and you live in a spiritual world. In spirit, there is no time except that which you give it. Stop saying, "I am getting older." You are not worshiping God, only time when you make that statement.
Affirmation:

> "So that youth is renewed like the eagle's" (Psalm 103:5, King James Version). I am youthful.

Affirmation:

> "Let his flesh become fresh with youth; let him return to the days of his youthful vigor" (Job 33:25, Revised Standard Version). I am youthful.

Positive thinking and applying verses of the Bible regenerate your body and life. Who do you want to believe? God? Or what society is saying? You live in a universe that is governed by law and principle, and there is a principle of youth and life.

12. Entertainment

"A cheerful heart is a good medicine; but a downcast spirit dries up the bones." (Proverbs 17:22) In order to stay healthy, you need to take a vacation once in a while and keep yourself entertained. Life is to be lived. You can't save it. In fifty-five years, I have seen plenty of sick people in my profession because all they ever do is work. They have no interest in doing anything joyful, and they take life too seriously.

You have control over all of the issues listed here. Put them to work for you. You can't buy health at any price, but you can help yourself stay healthy.

Health and the Spiritual Side of You

You live in God's world, which is spiritual and mental. The word you speak is spirit and reproduces after its kind in due time. "Death and Life are in the power of the tongue, and those who love it will eat its fruits" (Proverbs 18:22, King James Version).

Every time you say something about yourself, you are speaking death or life. Jesus Christ said that you are to be perfect even as your Father in heaven is perfect. If you are to be perfect as the Father in heaven is perfect, what are you saying about yourself or someone else that is contrary to that statement? Stop making negative statements about yourself. Only make positive statements about yourself to help keep you healthy and full of joy. Affirm and apply the following verse and affirmations in your daily life.

1. "Who forgives all your inequity, who heals all your diseases" (Psalm 103:3, King James Version).
2. I was healed by His sacrifice.
3. I am healed, whole and perfect, as the Father in heaven is perfect.
4. I am healthy. There is a principle of health.
5. I am happy and full of joy.
6. God is my health and my conscience.

You are spiritual; and if you want good health, a clear conscience is a requirement. That is why you have to read the Bible yourself so you will know what is right and wrong. You have a physical and spiritual body. "If there is a physical body, there is also a spiritual body, but it is not the spiritual which is first, but the physical and then the spiritual" (1 Corinthians 15:44, King James Version).

The spirit of God is inside you, through you, and around you. You are governed by law and principle. Because you can't see the law doesn't mean it's not there. If you go against the law, you will punish yourself until you change to the positive side of life.

"The fear of the Lord leads to life; and he who has it rests satisfied; he will not be visited by harm" (Proverbs 19:23, King James Version). God said that he would be the conscience and health of his people. You live in God's world. You have to speak the words, "I am healthy." We have been pretty much taught, "I will believe it when I see it." That is not how the law and principle of life works. You must speak the word first (I am healthy), then do whatever it takes to maintain health before it becomes a reality.

Spiritual body

The spiritual body is the real you and connects you with the invisible world on one side and the physical and material world on the other side. The spiritual body is your soul, what holds you up. Without the spiritual body, you would be just like a glob of jelly on the floor. That is why you need to read the Bible so you will know what to do to protect your soul.

I have been going for acupuncture treatments for over thirty-five years. If you want to see how the spirit flows through your body, I recommend you read a book on acupuncture. Then you will have a better understanding of how the spirit moves through your body and how it affects your life.

Christ Jesus within You

If you don't realize that Christ Jesus is within you and that you are controlled by law and principle, you are missing one of the most important parts that the Bible has been trying to tell you. That is why Jesus Christ is your Lord and Savior. He will help you regenerate your body and your life. Christ Jesus will also help you solve your problems and help you achieve your goals. Some people think if they accept Jesus as their Lord and Savior that they are going to heaven. That is only the beginning. Christ Jesus is within you now to help you with your goals.

Jesus did not come to prepare you for death but to prepare you for life now. The life principle is eternal now, not just in the by and by. You are now alive to God through Christ Jesus. Learn to follow your intuition, that inner feeling. That is how God informs you and helps to protect your health.

Affirmation:

God is among the living, not the dead.

You operate from the inside out. The way you think, talk, and act has a great impact on your health. Your word reproduces after its kind in due time. To protect your health, make these positive affirmations:

- I am happy and full of joy.
- I am healed, whole, and as perfect as the Father in heaven is perfect.
- I am healthy.
- I am youthful.

Do not let the word of life depart from your mouth. Take the verses from the Bible and apply them to your life. This is a very important point to remember. The word you speak has control over the flesh. You are the captain of your life when you learn to control your thinking and only think positively about all things. If you follow Jesus Christ's sayings, he will lead you to the correct way of thinking, talking, and acting. He will lead you to the way the universe and you, as a part of it, were meant to function in the first place.

You have four choices when it comes to the law and principle of life:

1. Don't believe the law exists and do nothing.
2. Just follow whatever society does and believes.
3. Just don't care.

4. Follow Jesus Christ and believe that the law and principle exist, putting it to work for you by faith.

"For God shows no partiality" (Romans 2:11, King James Version). In other words, God doesn't care who you are. The law works the same for everyone. That is why you need to read the Bible yourself. You need to understand what is right and wrong for you to maintain good health.

Points to remember:

1. The Bible is your manual to good health. Read it and apply the verses.
2. You have a physical and spiritual body.
3. Affirm: I am healthy.
4. You should know what every pill you are taking is for.
5. Negative thinking is destructive for your health.
6. Positive thinking helps you to heal and to maintain your health.
7. Don't let illegal drugs destroy your life. Get high on life. Help someone or get a new interest.
8. Your entertainment and vacations are very important for good health.
9. A cheerful heart is a good medicine, but a downcast spirit dries up the bones.
10. The spirit has control over the flesh.
11. Christ Jesus is within you now.
12. Jesus Christ is your Lord and Savior now, not just in the by and by.
13. You operate from the inside out by the word you speak.
14. God shows no partiality.
15. Sleep is a habit. Set your goal to go to bed and get up at a designated time. Stay with your set timer.

God is Life

God is life, omnipresent and eternal now. Adam introduced death into the world by his sin—wrong thinking, talking, and action. That has led man to start thinking wrongly, against the way the universe and you were created to function. Wrong thinking goes against the instructions found in the Bible.

The universe has a positive and a negative side to it.

Fig. 1

(+)	Positive	Good	Life	Regeneration
(-)	Negative	Evil	Death	Destruction

God's power is on the positive side of life and has the power to overcome the negative issues of life. Sin means you are thinking the wrong way and going against the way your mental powers were created to function. This leads to death. If you are not connected to the spiritual world, you have no way to regenerate your body and life.

The Universe You Live In

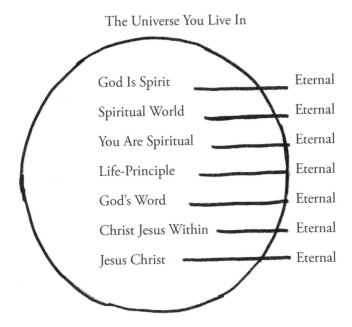

Each one of these items in Fig. 2 is eternal now. Each has a direct effect on your life. The question is, if you live in a spiritual world where the life principle is eternal now, why do you grow old and die? It is because people believe you are supposed to. They look at their parents, and that is how they gauge their lifespan. Start looking at your spiritual father in heaven. His life span is eternal. The New Testament covenant by God through Jesus Christ came to show the life principle and to promote life over death

Affirmations:

1. "I am come that they may have life and have it more abundantly" (John 10:10, King James Version).
2. Do not let the word of life depart from your mouth.
3. "I am the resurrection and the Life. He that believes in me, though he dies yet he will live, and he who lives and believes in me shall never die" (John 11:25, King James Version).

Many people have believed Psalm 90:10. "The years of our life are threescore and ten" (King James Version). That does not apply to you or anyone else unless you believe it. That is not in the New Testament. Remember John 3:16, "For God so loved the world that He gave His only son, that whoever believes in Him should not perish but have eternal life."

I have been working with the general public through the salon for over fifty-five years and have had many clients who were in their eighties and nineties. I even had one over one hundred years old. So as you can see, the passage does not apply to you or to anyone else who understands that we are spiritual beings living in a spiritual world. Most people have a carnal mind, and they follow what society believes about life and longevity on earth, which is not based on the truth.

From the time you were born, you have been programmed by what you have heard from family, friends, television, doctors, etc. Just because some of the people you have known have died does not change the truth—the life principle is here now, and you can speak the word of life to yourself. You cannot think of death and life at the same time. Which do you choose? I hope life.

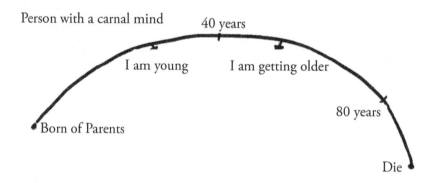

From the time you are born until now, you have been hearing, "You are getting older." Hearing this and saying it to yourself is negative, causing you to restrict the flow of life through you.

Also when you say, "I am a year older," it has the same effect. You are not material; you are spiritual. And in spirit, there is no time.

When you make statements like that, you are not worshiping God; you are worshiping time. There is no time in spirit except that which you give it. Jesus Christ came to help you renew your body and life.

You are born of god.

Your Body Is Spiritual and
Continuously Regenerating

If you understand that you are spiritual and born of God and that your body and life are continuously regenerating themselves, then you will have control over your mental process. This will give you great power over your life. The Christ Jesus within you knows how to achieve the end result of your problems or of the goals you have set.

One of your goals should be to seek eternal life now. By following Jesus Christ, you will find righteousness and positivity through thought, word, and action. You need to read your Bible so you will know what is right and wrong for you. People will stop living longer when they realize that they are spiritual and stop thinking about getting older and dying. They need to begin thinking about youth and eternal life now, not in the afterworld.

Affirmations:

1. "Thy youth is renewed like the eagle's" (Psalm 103:5, King James Version). I am youthful.
2. "Thou shall decree a thing, and it will be established unto you" (Job 22:28, King James Version).

You have a choice. You can follow society, get older, and die. Or you can follow Jesus Christ, remain youthful and full of life. Only you can do your own thinking and reap the benefits by applying the Word. You speak to yourself. When you use the affirmations throughout this book, you are becoming a doer of the Word.

Points to remember:

1. God is life, omnipresent and eternal, flowing through you now.
2. Adam introduced death into the world by his sin—wrong thinking, talking, and actions.
3. Jesus Christ within you is your Lord and Savior who came to overcome death for you and to introduce eternal life for everyone.
4. The universe has a positive and negative side to it. Only think positive thoughts.
5. Through Christ Jesus, God's power is on the positive side of life.
6. Sin and evil equal negative, wrong thought, speech, and action.
7. You will find your help on the positive side of life.
8. There is a Principle of Life that flows through you now.
9. You live in a universe that is spiritual and mental. There is no time in spirit. Stop saying, "I am getting older." Say, "Thy youth is renewed like that of the eagle's. I am youthful."
10. You now live by the New Testament covenant through Christ Jesus.
11. The affirmations from the Bible are to help you to regenerate your body and life.
12. You can live longer in good health when you accept Christ Jesus as your Lord and Savior, realize that you are spiritual, and believe in eternal life now.
13. Stop making negative statements about yourself that are not based on truth.
14. A carnal mind leads to death; and spiritual mind renews and regenerates the body, leading to life.

15. God's words are alive and creative. Speak God's words to your life: "I am youthful. I am full of life. I am strong."

16. If you say, "I am getting older," you are not worshipping God; you are worshipping time.

17. You are born of God, eternal and spiritual now.

18. Your body is in continuous regeneration. Only speak positive suggestions to yourself.

19. You are master of your own soul when you understand how your mental power works.

20. No one can think for you. Only you can speak your own word. Keep it on the positive side of life.

21. You have to apply God's Word. Affirm: "I am youthful, etc.," before you reap the benefits.

22. When you apply your affirmations and verses from the Bible (for example, "I am strong. I can do all things through Christ who strengthens me"), you are becoming a doer of the Word. As stated in James 1:22, "I am a doer of the word and not a hearer only" (King James Version).

23. You live in a sea of spirit that controls your life by law and principle. The fear of the Lord is the beginning of knowledge.

24. "For to be carnally minded is death, but to be spiritual minded is Life and Peace" (Romans 8:6, King James Version).

Not by Faith Alone

> You see that a man is justified by works and not by faith only. (James 2:24, Revised Standard Version)

You must become a doer of the Word. For example, take a steak. I could tell you what ranch the beef grew up one, what feed lot it was sent to, and what type of grain it was fed. I could tell you where the beef was slaughtered and the name of the butcher. I could tell you the vitamins found in the steak and the benefits they have for your body and health. All of that information would mean nothing unless you ate the steak. The same is true about all of the information and truths you have learned up to now. It all means nothing unless you apply the information to your daily life, becoming a doer of the Word.

Spiritual and Mental Universe

1. The real world is spiritual and invisible.
2. You live in a spiritual world.
3. The universe has a positive and negative side.
4. The law and principle
5. You are a spiritual being.
6. You possess certain mental powers.
7. The world was created by spoken word. You have to create your world by your spoken word.
8. The law of attraction
9. Every living thing comes from the invisible to the visible, including you.

10. The principle of life is eternal.
11. Jesus Christ within you is your Lord and Savior now.
12. God is life eternal.
13. Adam introduced death into the world.
14. Jesus Christ overcame death and introduced eternal Life.
15. You must be born again.

Just like in the example of the steak, knowing all that information means nothing unless you use it. Memorize the affirmations and verses from the Bible and apply them to your daily life. In other words, you must become a doer of the Word in your life.

> What does it profit my brethren if a man says he has faith, but has not works. (James 2:14, King James Version)
> You see that a man is justified by works and not faith alone. (James 2:24, King James Version)
> But be doers of the word and not hearers only. (James 6:22, King James Version)
> Now faith is the substance of things hoped for, the evidence of things not seen. (Hebrews 11:1, King James Version)

The scripture states in Deuteronomy 8:3, "You will not live by bread alone, but every word from God's mouth." You are speaking God's word here on earth; and every word you speak through Christ Jesus within is going to reproduce after its kind in due time, be it a positive or a negative statement. This is why you must read the Bible yourself if you are going to be a doer of the Word and apply the Word in your life.

"Faith is the substance hoped for, the evidence of things not seen." What do you hope for? Car? House? Spouse? Job? You are using faith every time you speak.

Fig. 1

Faith	Positive	Love	I Am Happy	I Am Youthful
Belief	Negative	Hate	I Am Depressed	I Am Getting Old

Faith and belief go together. You are using faith when you make the statement, "I am happy and full of joy." If you keep making that statement to yourself, it will become a habit and a positive belief. You are going to have to decide whether you want to believe what your friends, family, and society are saying about life or whether you have faith and believe in what God has to say about you.

When you become a doer of the Word, you should remember that there are four different parts to your life that must consider.

The Four Different Parts of Your Life

1. The spiritual side of you
2. Your mental powers
3. The physical (body) side of you
4. The material side of you (house, car, spouse, etc.)

Universe

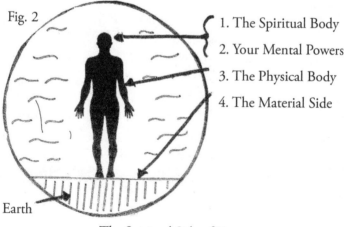

Fig. 2

1. The Spiritual Body
2. Your Mental Powers
3. The Physical Body
4. The Material Side

Earth

The Spiritual Side of You

The Bible is your spiritual guide to live by. God is spirit and truth. You have to worship God. There are many aspects of God. By meditating on the different aspects of God, you can make them a part of your life.

Life

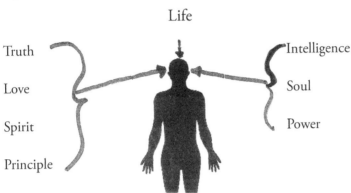

Truth

Love

Spirit

Principle

Intelligence

Soul

Power

Each of these aspects is guided by law and principle. They reproduce after their kind in your life, the spiritual side.

A.   Jesus Christ within you is your Lord and Savior.
B.   The universe is invisible, spiritual and mental.
C.   The spirit of God is in you, through you, and around you.
D.   You are spiritual and eternal now.
E.   You must be born again in spirit and truth.
F.   The spirit has control over your flesh.
G.   God's word is eternal.

For the law of the Spirit of Life in Christ Jesus has made me free from the law in sin and death. "When the spirit of truth comes, He will guide you into all the truth" (John 16:13, Revised Standard Version). This is just a small list of information about your spiritual side.

Your Mental Powers

Affirmations:

1. "As a man thinketh in his heart so is he" (Proverbs 23:7, King James Version).
2. "Do not be conformed to this world, but be transformed by the renewing of your mind" (Romans 12:2, King James Version).
3. Do not let the word of life depart from your mouth.
4. I can do all things through Christ who strengthens me.
5. "I am come that they may have life and have it more abundantly" (John 10:10, King James Version).
6. I am happy and full of joy.
7. "Let my flesh become fresh with youth; let me return to my youthful vigor" (Job 33:25, King James Version).
8. "There is no condemnation in them that are in Christ Jesus" (Romans 8:1, King James Version).
9. "If any man be in Christ, he is a new creation. Old things have passed away; all things have become new" (2 Corinthians 5:17, King James Version).
10. I am full of life.
11. "God is love. He that abideth in love abideth in God and God abideth in him" (1 John 4:16, King James Version).
12. "If you confess with your lips that Jesus is Lord and believe in your heart that God raised Him from the dead, you will be saved" (Romans 10:9, King James Version).
13. It is the Lord that giveth you the power to get wealth. I am wealthy and rich.
14. The Father and I are one.

Use these affirmations in your life and keep expanding. When you realize that the word you speak is your seed, you will reap what you sow. You should take control of your thinking and only make positive affirmations to yourself. Remember that the law of attraction is always working for or against you.

Fig. 5

Positive	Law of Attraction	For Good
Negative		Against Evil

As you read the Scripture and apply the different verses, think positively about everything. That is how your mental powers were created to function.

The Physical Side of You

Spiritual World You Live In

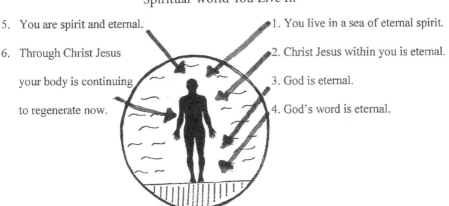

5. You are spirit and eternal.

6. Through Christ Jesus your body is continuing to regenerate now.

1. You live in a sea of eternal spirit.

2. Christ Jesus within you is eternal.

3. God is eternal.

4. God's word is eternal.

1. You live in a spiritual and mental universe that is eternal.
2. Christ Jesus within you is your Lord and Savior now and is eternal.
3. You live in the spirit of God. He is in you, through you, and around you. The spirit of
4. God is eternal now.
5. God's word is eternal.
6. The real you is spiritual and eternal now.
7. Through Christ Jesus within you, your body is in the process of regenerating now.

My question to you is, why do you believe your body is getting older each day? Your belief does not coincide with the truth about you. You have to separate your body from the time you have spent on earth. Your body is not the same age as your chronological age. Your body is not material but spiritual and in the process of regenerating. You build age into your body by what you keep suggesting to yourself and your belief about age. "I am getting older. I am old." These statements are not based on the truth.

Affirmations:

A. "Thy youth is renewed like that of the eagle's" (Psalm 103:5, King James Version).
B. I am youthful.
C. "Let my flesh become fresh with youth. Let me return to my youthful vigor" (Job 33:25, King James Version).

You have to decide. Do you want to follow your friends, family, and society? Or do you want to believe what God says about you? Let me remind you that God's word is alive and eternal.

Affirmations:

A. "The grass withers, the flowers fade, but the word of our God stands forever" (Isaiah 40:8, King James Version).
B. "As a man thinketh in his heart so is he" (Proverbs 23:7, King James Version).
C. "Thou shall decree a thing, and it will be established unto you" (Job 22:28, King James Version).
D. "Be ye transformed by renewing your mind" (Romans 12:2, King James Version).

When you read a verse, make it personal. For example, say, "I am transformed by renewing my mind." The number one mistake that people make is that they use positive thinking for success, wealth, money, and careers. But they make negative statements about their physical bodies, themselves, and their lives. Become a doer of the Word and only speak on the positive side of life. You live in God's world. You have to speak the word by faith before you get a positive result. Say, "I can do all things through Christ who strengthens me."

Affirmations:

A. Bless your eyes. Through Christ, I see clearly and perfectly as the Father in heaven is perfect.
B. Bless your ears: Through Christ, I hear clearly and perfectly as the Father in heaven is perfect.
C. Bless your age. I am youthful.
D. Bless your hair. I have thick hair.
E. Bless your skin. I have firm, youthful skin.
F. Bless your strength. I am strong.
G. Bless your health. I am strong and healthy.
H. Bless your happiness. I am happy and full of joy.
I. Bless your Lord. I praise the Lord who hath made this day.
J. Bless your life. I will rejoice and be glad in it.

"Death and Life are in the Power of the tongue, and those who love it will eat its fruits" (Proverbs 18:21, Revised Standard Version).

If you are wise, you will only speak positive affirmations about your body and life. Become a thankful and grateful person, giving thanks to God for everything—for example, your youthfulness, your eyes, your ears, and your hair. Also, be thankful for Jesus Christ within you as your Lord and Savior.

The Material Side of You

The information beginning in Chapter 1 and throughout the book up until now brings us to this point. As they say, this is where the rubber meets the road. You must become a doer of the Word in order to achieve your personal goals and the necessities of your life—house, car, spouse, job, etc. God can only help you with your desires through Christ Jesus.

Spiritual Universe

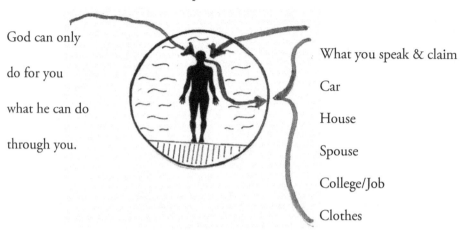

God can only do for you what he can do through you.

What you speak & claim
Car
House
Spouse
College/Job
Clothes

God can only help you with what he can do through you mentally. You control your own thinking. You have to claim that which you desire. All of what you have been learning up to this point, you are going to put together to work for you—your faith, I am, imagination, intuition, desire, and law of attraction.

Christ Jesus within you is your Lord and Savior. All power and authority have been given to Christ.

> Now faith is the substance of things hoped for,
> the evidence of things not seen. (Hebrews 11:1,
> King James Version)

Call these things that are not as if they were.

> And God said, Let there be light and there was
> light. (Genesis 1:3, King James Version)

That is an example you can follow. Let me remind you when you say, "I am," you are using God's name. Make sure you use it on the positive side of life. When you are trying to achieve a goal, get into the habit of writing out in detail what it is you want. God is only going to help when you know what you want. You would be surprised how many people don't really know what they want.

"Commit your work to the Lord, and your plans will be established" (Proverbs 16–3, King James Version). God knows ways that you do not know. The answer you are looking for might be found in a book, a person, an idea, or a place.

A Man or Woman Looking for a Spouse

As I have previously stated, I have worked with the general public for fifty-five years. In that time, I have seen many marriages—the good, the bad, and the ugly. It is no wonder that the divorce rate is over 50 percent for the first marriage and much higher for the second.

When I lived in Escondido, California, thirty years ago, a reporter I will call John worked at a local television station in San Diego. He decided to do research on couples who were about to get married. After one week, John decided that the couples spent more time kicking tires when they were looking for a car than they spent finding out about the person they were about to marry for a lifetime. Thirty years later, I now live in Clearwater, Florida. A reporter from Tampa, whom I will call Bill, decided to do a story about a couple planning to get married soon. After one week, Bill used exactly the same analogy that John had used thirty years before.

No wonder the divorce rate is so high. If you want a happy, lasting marriage, take some time to find out about the person you are planning to marry. After you get married, it's too late. You might find out that the love of your life is not the king or queen you thought he or she was.

Here is a list of questions you can use to help you to understand your prospective mate:

1. How and where does the person spend money? Money is the number one cause of problems in a marriage, many times leading to divorce. I have seen cases in which three

people couldn't support someone due to the way he or she spent money.

2. Do you want your husband or wife to also be your best friend? I have seen many couples who are unhappy because they never do anything together. They are husband and wife but not friends.

3. Do you want a person who likes to travel? I have known couples who were unhappy because one liked to travel and the other didn't. If they never went anywhere, one was happy but the other wasn't. If they traveled, there was still one unhappy partner.

4. Do you like sports? What kind?

5. Do you like going to movies? What type?

6. Do you like live theater?

7. Do you like to go to different attractions?

8. Where do you buy your clothes?

9. Do you like to travel by air?

10. Is the person you are about to marry a mama's boy or a daddy's girl? If so, you could be in competition with a family member, and this could spell trouble.

11. Does the person like to frequent bars?

12. Can you communicate easily with the other person?

13. What is the other person's opinion about the duties of the house? Lawn? Work?

14. Does the person have a drug or alcohol problem? Don't think that by marrying that type of person, you are going to help him or her. I have yet to see it work. Those people need professional help.

15. Never marry anyone with the idea that you are going to change that person. Accept the person as he or she is or move one.

16. Does the other person come from the same type of background? Small town? City?

17. Is the other person interested in going with you when you visit family? If not, this can be a problem in a marriage.

18. Do you agree on most important issues of life?
19. Has the person been married before? If so, are there any children involved? This can be a major problem in a second marriage. You should have rules set before you get married. Children, even as adults, can cause a lot of problems.
20. Is the person self-centered?
21. Does the person have a positive mental attitude?
22. What type of physical attributes do you prefer? Short? Tall? Heavy? Thin?
23. What type of climate does the person like? Cold or warm? This can be a major sticking point in a marriage. Living in the Sun Belt, I have seen this conflict many times. One spouse likes a warm climate, and the other likes a cold one. Someone is always unhappy.
24. Are there cultural differences?
25. Does the person have a good work ethic?
26. Does the person have high moral standards?

You can get all of these questions answered through casual conversation. You can say, "I am going to visit a friend or a family member. Do you ever travel?" Or "I am shopping this weekend at the mall. Where do you usually shop for clothes?"

Now, you might have noticed in the above questions, I did not mention love. That is because love is truly blind. It gets in the way of finding out about the other person. Some people think that love is going to solve all of their problems. However, it is not love that holds a marriage together. It is trust. I don't care how much you love someone. When the trust is broken over a period of time, love is going out the window, and your marriage will never be the same. A house divided will not stand.

I used to work in a spa that also housed a beauty salon. As I walked down the hall one day, I saw three young ladies in the tea room. They were all getting married within a week of each other. They asked me if I would give them my opinion of marriage. I asked them if they would allow me to say what I wanted to say before they spoke. They all agreed. I told them that that were ready to get married if they had figured out:

1. Who was going to mow the yard?
2. Who was going to clean the house?
3. Who was going to pay the bills?
4. Who was going to buy the food?
5. Who was going to do the banking?
6. Who was going to wash the dishes?
7. Who was going to do the laundry?
8. Who was going to cook?
9. After all of the bills were paid, what they were going to do with the money?

I told them that if they had all of this figured out, they were ready to get married. One of the girls jumped up and said, "You never said anything about love."

I told her that I had never seen love mow the grass, clean the house, or pay bills. I also told her that if she had to do all of the things I just mentioned by herself, her love would not survive. Love would soon turn to resentment.

Three weeks went by. On a Saturday, one of the girls came into the salon, laughing. I asked what happened. She said after she had been married one week, she and her husband sat down at the table to have dinner when she began to laugh. Her husband asked her what was so funny, and she told him that she was thinking about what I had said. As she looked around, there were dirty dishes in the sink, the lawn needed to be cut, and the house was dirty. They also needed to buy food; and after all of the bills were paid, there was very little money left to do anything. She had learned the reality of married life.

Love is only a part of the marriage formula. You have two personalities coming together with different desires and needs. The more things you have in common with each other, the stronger your marriage bond will be. Save yourself some future worry and problems by taking the time to decide the type of person you are looking for.

It is just as important to know what you don't want in a mate:

1. Someone who drinks too much
2. A person who constantly goes to bars
3. A party spirit
4. Someone who doesn't want to go anywhere or do anything
5. Someone who is negative
6. Someone who doesn't like to travel
7. Someone who spends money unwisely
8. Someone who doesn't want to work
9. Someone on drugs
10. Someone who is not kind and loving

You can add or subtract from this list based on your own likes and dislikes.

In the half century that I have worked with the general public, people of all income and education levels, I have found that the couples with the happiest marriages, some lasting forty to sixty years, all had one thing in common. Those who played together stayed together. In other words, these husbands and wives were also best friends.

Everyone has different desires and needs. To keep our marriage happy and strong, my wife and I had a policy that worked. It is a system that everyone can use to promote harmony in a marriage:

1. Every other year, my wife had to pick where she would like to go for vacation.
2. My wife chose every other movie we went to see.
3. Every other time we went out to dine, my wife chose the restaurant.
4. My wife chose every other live show at the theater.
5. When we were choosing an attraction to go to, my wife made the selection every other time.

This way, everyone gets what he or she desires. The needs of both spouses are met. This makes for a joyful marriage.

If you want God to help you get into the habit of writing out your goals so you have a clear picture of what you want, write them as if they were already reality.

Example:

I am happily married to a _____. (Fill in the type of person you would like to be married to.)

Use your "I am" (God's name).

Use your imagination, which is greater than positive knowledge, to see yourself doing things with the person you have written down. You used faith when you wrote down your description of your mate; and you are going to use your intuition (God speaking to you) so when you meet the right person, God will let you know by the right feeling. When you decide to get married, you bring in the law of attraction to help you find your mate.

After you have written out your goal and know the type of person you are looking for, pay attention to your intuition. You never know when or where you will meet that person—at a friend's wedding, while shopping, at a relative's house, on an airplane, at church, or through the internet. I once had a customer whom I will call Alice. Alice and a friend went to breakfast in a restaurant in Sarasota, Florida. A man I will call Joe was sitting by himself at a table. As Alice and her friend walked by Joe, Alice remarked that what he was eating looked good, and the two women walked to their table. After Joe finished eating, he came over and started talking to them. After a while, Joe told Alice that they should go out for coffee sometime. They exchanged phone numbers. Today Alice is still married to Joe, a multimillionaire. She said she didn't know what made her say something to Joe that morning. God knows what you want, and He knows how to get it. He might make you say or do something that you normally wouldn't.

Know what type of husband or wife you want. Act when that person comes into your life. Give thanks to God for your new mate as if it has already happened.

There Is More to Life than a Car and House

There is more to life than a car and house. What is your number one priority? To enjoy life to the fullest, let's look at the possibilities:

A. Travel
B. Theater
C. Attractions
D. Shows
E. Sports
F. Eating out
G. Cruises

I will use my personal experience in the next two segments so I can show you how things worked out for my wife and me. Anyone can do something in his or her life to get the most out of life.

Priorities

1. Travel
2. Car
3. House

Travel was the number one priority in our life. In order to do this, we bought two or three-year-old low-mileage cars, and our house was a size that fit our needs. That gave us the money we needed to travel for over forty-two years and to do all of the things that added to our fullness of life.

Buying a Car

If you want God to help you, you have to know what type of car you are looking for.

1. The model year (for example, 2016)
2. Buick, Chevy, Ford, etc.
3. Color

4. Type of interior (cloth or leather)
5. Price of car you can afford
6. Size of engine
7. Low mileage
8. One owner
9. No damage
10. Accessories (for example, electric seats, chrome wheels, etc.)

By buying this type of car, we saved from ten to fifteen thousand dollars over a new car. I only buy a used car at the dealership because they usually keep only the best-used cars. You can also use the same formula if you are looking for a new car. You have to do your part. Visit different dealers. Use your imagination and intuition to attract you to the car you are looking for. Be ready to extend your search area. We found our car at a dealership sixty-five miles from our home in Clearwater, Florida. As soon as I saw the car at the dealership in Sarasota, my intuition told me that this was the car. After we paid the price, taxes, and other fees, we had $1,538 left from the money we had allowed for the purchase. You can see it is very important that you know what you want if you expect God's help. Give thanks for His assistance.

Buying a House

A house is great if it is the proper size for your family and your needs. However, it can be a chain around your neck and become a problem if it takes too much of your money to live in and maintain it. In the last housing market boom, over six million home owners overpaid for their houses and went belly up when the market dropped. When buying a house, do not let fear force you into buying something you can't afford.

What You Should Consider when Buying a House

There are certain costs you need to consider when buying a home. Think about the monthly and yearly expenses. The size of the house should be not what you want but what your income will let you afford without taking all of your paycheck. You will need enough money for other living costs. When you are looking for a house, you can estimate the cost the following:

A. Normal living cost of a house

1. Electric bill
2. Water and sewage
3. Garbage
4. Phone
5. Taxes
6. Insurance
7. Lawn Service
8. Cable
9. Club fees
10. Flood insurance
11. Heating

B. Basic living cost:

1. Food
2. Health insurance
3. Car repair
4. Credit cards
5. Cell phone
6. Computer
7. Church
8. Gasoline
9. Gas for home
10. School costs
11. College
12. Life insurance
13. Dental
14. Medical
15. Newspapers

16. Children's needs
17. Clothing
18. Pets

C. Things that make life enjoyable

1. Movies
2. Live theater
3. Vacations
4. Weekend travel
5. Charity
6. Restaurants
7. Sports
8. Clubs
9. Day trips
10. Festivals
11. Attractions
12. State Fairs
13. Camping
14. Hiking

Now you have to figure the maintenance cost of your home as time goes by.

1. Replace air conditioning/heating
2. Replace hot-water heater
3. Replace the roof
4. Repaint inside and out
5. Maintain the yard and plants

The cost of each of these items will go up a little each year. Therefore, it is important to select a size of house, whether it be 1,200 or 1,800 square feet, that is best suited for your family income. You shouldn't put too much money into your house payment. Don't allow your payments to be so high that you have no money left for the things that make life a joy.

Write out your affirmation: I own a _____
(Type of house you are looking for.) Then start looking at the different areas that have the size of house you need. Commit this work to the Lord.

There are several ways to buy a house:

1. Rent to buy
2. Buy from the owner
3. A repossessed house
4. A foreclosure house
5. Buy a new house
6. Take over someone's payments. If you were to buy this type of house, make sure you can refinance without penalties.

Types of Mortgages

There are different types of loans—fifteen, twenty, and thirty-year. Keep one thing in mind. You need a loan that is fixed as long as you can get the mortgage so your payments will be low enough for you to have money left for living expenses. Make sure you get a loan that allows you to pay more if your income should increase, paying it off without a penalty. My wife and I got a thirty-year mortgage on our house. When we started drawing our social security, we still worked and paid off our house in fifteen years. By doing it this way, we had more money to enjoy life.

Do your homework before you buy any house. I have seen many couples buy their dream house; and within two or three years, they are in trouble with their payments. Many times it is because their insurance has gone up anywhere from three to seven thousand dollars in one year. They have to sell their house and move out of the state to an area where they can afford to buy a house and live within their income.

Affirmation:

"I can do all things through Christ which strengthen me" (Philippians 4:13, King James

Version). Again, when you write any of your goals, state them in a positive way. Call those things that are not as if they were!

Points to remember:

1. Faith apart from work is dead.
2. Information means nothing unless it is applied.
3. Call those things that are not as if they were.
4. You can do all things through Christ who strengthens you.
5. The law of attraction is always working for or against you.
6. There are four different parts to you: spiritual, mental, physical, and material.
7. God can only do for you what he can do through you mentally.
8. Get in the habit of writing out your goals.
9. Commit your work to God.
10. Marriage should not be a battleground.
11. Know what kind of person you want to marry.
12. The long-lasting marriages are the ones in which the husband and wife are best friends.
13. Never try to change anyone; accept your spouse as he or she is.
14. There is more to enjoy in life than having a car and house.
15. Write out your priorities.
16. "Commit your work to the Lord and your thoughts will be established" (Proverbs 16:3, King James Version).
17. If buying a used car, it is best to buy at the dealership.
18. When buying a home, buy the size of house you need and can afford.
19. Before buying a house, figure out how much it is going to cost you to live there.

Conclusion

The Bible is your spiritual guide to read and study. It will provide instructions and wisdom to live by. If you turn this knowledge into action and always walk on the positive side, applying the truth to your life, you will be filled with the love and happiness God has meant for you.

References

Bibles

The Holy Bible: King James Version.
The Holy Bible: Revised Standard Edition.

Books

Anderson, U. S. *Three Magic Words*. New York: Thomas Nelson & Son, 1954.

Bristol, Claude M. and Howard Herman. *TNT: The Power within You*. Englewood Cliffs, NJ:

Prentice-Hall, 1954.

Butterworth, Eric. *The Universe is Calling*. Kansas City, Missouri: Unity House-Harper One, 1993.

Fillmore, Charles. *Christian Healing*. Kansas City, Missouri: Unity Books, 1909.

Fillmore, Myrtle. *Myrtle Fillmore's Healing Letters*. Kansas City, MO: Unity Books, 1890.

Fox, Emmet. *Power through Constructive Thinking*. San Francisco: Harper & Row, 1932.

———. *The Mental Equivalent*. Kansas City, Missouri: Unity Courtyard Books, 1943.

———. *The Sermon on the Mount*. San Francisco: Harper & Row, 1934.

———. *The Ten Commandments*. San Francisco: Harper & Row, 1953.

Goldsmith, Joel S. *Beyond Words and Thoughts*. Santa Barbara, California: Acropolis Books, 1968.

———. *Consciousness Unfolding*. Santa Barbara, California: Acropolis Books, 1962.

Haanel, Charles. *Mental Chemistry.* St. Louis, Missouri: Charles F. Haanel Publishing, 1922.

———. *The Master Key System.* St. Louis, Missouri: The Master Key Institute, 1912.

Hill, Napoleon. *Think and Grow Rich.* Monica, California: Wilshire Book Company, 1937.

Holmes, Ernest. *Creative Mind and Success.* New York: Dodd, Mead, and Company, 1965.

———. *It's Up to You.* Los Angeles, California: Science of Mind Publications, 1968.

———. *Science of Mind.* New York: Dodd, Mead, and Company, 1938.

Holmes, Ernest and Willis Kinnear. *Thoughts Are Things.* Los Angeles, California: Science of Mind
Publications, 1967.

King, Godfre Ray. *The "I Am" Discourses.* Schaumburg, Illinois: Saint Germain Foundation, 1935.

Maltz, Maxwell. *Psycho-Cybernetics.* Englewood Cliffs, New Jersey: Prentice-Hall, 1960.

Mathews, Arthur Guy. *Take It Easy.* New York: Sheridan House, 1945.

Murphy, Joseph. *The Miracle of Mind Dynamics.* Englewood Cliffs, New Jersey: Prentice-Hall, 1964.

———. *The Power of Your Subconscious Mind.* Englewood Cliffs, New Jersey: Prentice-Hall, 1963.

Peale, Norman Vincent. *The Power of Positive Thinking.* New York: Prentice-Hall, 1952.

Troward, Thomas. *Bible Mysteries and Bible Meaning.* New York: Dodd, Mead, and Company, 1913.

———. *The Edinburgh Lectures on Mental Science.* New York: Dodd, Mead, and Company, 1909.

———. *The Hidden Power.* New York: Classic Books International, 2010.

————. *The Law and the Word.* New York: Dodd, Mead, and Company, 1917.

Schindler, John A. *How to Live 365 Days a Year.* Englewood Cliffs, New Jersey: Prentice-Hall, 1954.

Louie Van Greninger, a native of Oklahoma, grew up on a farm with his parents and nine siblings. After serving in the navy, he graduated from the Marion County Vocational Beauty School in Ocolo, Florida, before continuing his education in Canada and Oklahoma. For over fifty years, he has worked as a hairstylist in five different states, establishing a loyal clientele from all walks of life. Greninger's first book was entitled *How to Use Psychology in Your Salon and Community*. A widower, he  resides in Clearwater, Florida, where he continues to work.

CPSIA information can be obtained
at www.ICGtesting.com
Printed in the USA
FSHW020258251019
63329FS